A KWANZAA KEEPSAKE AND COOKBOOK

Celebrating the Holiday with Family, Community, and Tradition

Previously published as *A Kwanzaa Keepsake:*
Celebrating the Holiday with New Traditions and Feasts

JESSICA B. HARRIS

SCRIBNER
New York   London   Toronto   Sydney   New Delhi

Scribner
An Imprint of Simon & Schuster, LLC
1230 Avenue of the Americas
New York, NY 10020

First Scribner hardcover edition November 2024

Previously published as *A Kwanzaa Keepsake: Celebrating the Holiday with New Traditions and Feasts.*

SCRIBNER and design are trademarks of Simon & Schuster, LLC

Simon & Schuster: Celebrating 100 Years of Publishing in 2024

For information about special discounts for bulk purchases, please contact
Simon & Schuster Special Sales at 1-866-506-1949 or business@simonandschuster.com.

The Simon & Schuster Speakers Bureau can bring authors to your live event. For more information
or to book an event, contact the Simon & Schuster Speakers Bureau at 1-866-248-3049
or visit our website at www.simonspeakers.com.

Interior design by Davina Mock-Maniscalco

Manufactured in the United States of America

10 9 8 7 6 5 4 3 2 1

Library of Congress Cataloging-in-Publication Data has been applied for.

ISBN 978-1-6680-3586-3
ISBN 978-1-6680-3587-0 (ebook)

DEDICATION

I celebrated my first Kwanzaa in the home of friends in Bedford Stuyvesant, Brooklyn, in New York City in the 1980s. The celebration was small and the three younger children in the family were thrilled to be participating in the ceremony. The son, a bright young child, eyes gleaming with thoughts of the holiday, lit the candle and spoke briefly yet movingly about the Kujichagulia—self-determination. I was touched, and vowed to celebrate the holiday in my own small way even though I have no children of my own.

By the time that I penned those words in 1995, that bright young man-child was dead, killed by what was then escalating random street violence. In the intervening almost thirty years, violence against young Black Americans has become an epidemic in this country, and we seemingly are backsliding into a morass of hatred and fear.

Today, *A Kwanzaa Keepsake and Cookbook* remains for the memory of that young man and also for all those Black American youths whose lives have been cut short and whose promise left unfulfilled. It is also for the living and for Black American children and parents everywhere.

It is for all those who have gone before who made our lives—all our lives—better and brighter, especially those who moved us forward as a people.

It is for all those here and now who work to make our lives—all of our lives—better, brighter, and more equitable.

It is for all of those yet to come. May the battles of yesterday be over. May the conflicts of today end. May the principles of Kwanzaa reinforce the values of our families and make this world better and brighter for us all.

CONTENTS

FOREWORD

CARLA HALL

I t's with great pleasure that I write this foreword for *A Kwanzaa Keepsake and Cookbook*, a book ingrained with the wisdom and warmth of its author, Dr. Jessica B. Harris.

My first introduction to Jessica's written work was in 2005 while I was working as a private chef in the Bahamas. *Sky Juice and Flying Fish: Tastes of a Continent*, with its approachable recipes and, more importantly, its cultural insights, were instrumental to my journey and success at that time. That book became a talisman, guiding and connecting me with my clients by offering authentic culinary experiences.

Our paths crossed more personally in 2017, the year I had the privilege of interviewing Jessica for her memoir, *My Soul Looks Back*. That evening, her vibrant and evocative storytelling told in her resonant voice transported me to different times and places. That encounter blossomed into a friendship that we have continued to nourish with shared meals and memories.

Some of those memories revealed surprising connections between us. I once recounted to Jessica the story of my culinary awakening in Paris in the late eighties. The expat Sunday brunches I attended were hosted and prepared by Elaine Evans, a Memphis native. As I shared my fond memories of those gatherings, Jessica revealed that she too knew Elaine—the two of them were friends and Jessica had a role in shaping Elaine's culinary skills. In that moment we realized that years before we ever met, the Universe had already connected us.

A Kwanzaa Keepsake and Cookbook is about honoring connections such as these over multiple generations. Through the tradition of her impactful story-telling, Jessica invites us to weave our own family histories into the rich tapestry of Kwanzaa's origins, principles, and its potential to nurture community, reflection, and personal growth. This book stands out not only as a guide to celebrating Kwanzaa but as a beacon of Jessica's ability to intertwine historical depth with contemporary significance, making sure to include overlooked pillars in the Black community. Her narrative, both enlightening and enriching, acts as a lens through which we can examine our lives and the fabric of our communities.

Embarking on the journey through *A Kwanzaa Keepsake and Cookbook*, readers are offered a chance to deepen their understanding of Kwanzaa and its enduring relevance in their own families. It is meant to be a living, breathing token of a family's legacy—the families we're born into and the ones we choose ourselves. I am honored to recommend this book, and certain that Jessica's insights will not only inspire but resonate deeply, just as her friendship and scholarly contributions have enriched my life. *A Kwanzaa Keepsake and Cookbook* is a testament to the connections and shared histories that shape our experiences, underlining the power of stories to forge bonds and illuminate paths—whether previously traveled or yet to come.

AUTHOR'S NOTE

As I picked up my slightly battered copy of *A Kwanzaa Keepsake,* I first turned to the acknowledgments page and was appalled by the number of friends that have passed into eternity. Now, almost thirty years after the original publication, I must begin by honoring their memories and first among them my mother who died in 2000. My father had already passed into ancestorship before this book was written. Today I am heartened by the fact that I am still in contact with many of the others and even more thrilled by the fact that new friends keep coming.

WHAT IS KWANZAA?

Those who think that holidays are days steeped in centuries-old tradition are always surprised to hear that the Black American feast of Kwanzaa was established in 1966. That was the year Maulana Karenga decided that Black Americans needed a time of cultural reaffirmation. He looked east to Africa, East Africa, and came up with a celebration that is a compilation of several harvest festivals and celebrations that are held throughout the continent. The name *Kwanzaa* comes from the Swahili word *kwanza*, meaning "first," as in the phrase *matunda ya kwanza* ("first fruits"). The second "a" distinguishes the Black American *kwanzaa* from the African *kwanza*. A most likely apocryphal tale is told that during one of the early Kwanzaa celebrations, a children's pageant was held, with each child holding up a card with the letters of the word *kwanza*, which at that time was spelled with one "a." One child was left letterless and weeping at the end of the row. A second "a" was quickly produced, the day was saved, and the holiday was forever after known as Kwanzaa.

Occurring annually from December 26 to January 1, Kwanzaa is a time of feasting, and of self-examination. It was at first celebrated mainly by cultural nationalists who wished to express their Pan-African solidarity. Yet, as word of the new holiday and its family-strengthening virtues spread, Black Americans from all walks of life began to celebrate the seven nights of reflection. In 2009, according to the American Cultural Center, thirty million people of all political leanings and in all walks of life celebrated the holiday, one of the fastest growing in the history of the world; those numbers have decreased slightly over the years, but with the growing popularity of Juneteenth, Kwanzaa is experiencing a resurgence. The roots of Kwanzaa are in Africa, but the fruits of the tree are truly Black American. Ironically, some of its branches are reaching back to the motherland from which it sprang, as Kwanzaa is celebrated in more and more countries from the Caribbean to Brazil to Europe in places where people from the African diaspora are present.

Although Kwanzaa is celebrated at the end of the year like the Christian celebration of Christmas, the Hindu celebration of Diwali, the Jewish celebration of Chanukah, and traditional European New Year's celebrations, it is not designed as an alternative to or replacement for any of those holidays. Kwanzaa may be celebrated jointly with any or all the year-end holidays. More importantly, it also offers a time for reflection and self-affirmation, in contrast with the rampant commercialization that has overtaken some of the other holidays. It must be noted, though, that some of that has changed and Kwanzaa, too, has become commercialized. There are now US Post Office Kwanzaa stamps, Kwanzaa cards from Hallmark, and the holiday has been recognized by larger commercial entities as a way of niche marketing to Black Americans. Traditional celebrants ignore all of that and hew to the original idea of the holiday by supporting Black American businesses and creating homemade gifts.

The celebration of Kwanzaa is guided by the Nguzo Saba or Seven Principles. Each day of the weeklong festival is devoted to the celebration of one of these building blocks of self-awareness.

Umoja	Unity
Kujichagulia	Self-Determination
Ujima	Collective Work and Responsibility
Ujamaa	Cooperative Economics
Nia	Purpose
Kuumba	Creativity
Imani	Faith

The mystical number seven is at the core of the celebration: There are seven days, seven principles, and even seven symbols of the festival. The symbols are the *mazao*, the fruits and vegetables of the harvest that are a part of the celebration table; the *mkeka*, the placemat on which they are arranged; and the *kinara*, the seven-branched candlestick that holds the red, black, and green candles, the *mishumaa saba*, that are lighted each evening. There are also the *muhindi*, the ears of corn that represent each child still remaining at home; the *kikombe cha umoja*, the chalice of unity from which the ceremonial libation is poured (post Covid, the days of sipping from a communal chalice are for the most part over); and the *zawadi*, the gifts.

Kwanzaa is essentially a family holiday, whether it be nuclear family, extended family, or communal family. Each evening of the holiday, family members gather around the celebration table to read the Seven Principles and meditate on the principle of the day while the leader of the ceremony lights one of the candles. Visitors are asked to participate as the nightly ceremony is held, the candles lighted, and the libation poured from the communal cup.

There are as many different types of Kwanzaa as there are types of families in the Black American community. Black Americans are known for improvisation; our virtuoso turns have created musical forms that have made the entire world sing and dance. Our artistic endeavors have redefined Western art forms. Wherever we have stepped and stopped, our transformational and improvisational skills have changed the country and the hemisphere. Our expressions are found in domains as wide-ranging as cooking, music, and language to mention but a few. In our world, there's always room for improvisation; it would be impossible for us not to improvise on the themes of Kwanzaa.

So, we ring in changes and create new riffs on our own holiday. There are single Kwanzaas, celebrated by individuals with friends and neighbors; nuclear family Kwanzaas with mommy, daddy, and the kids gathering each evening to light the candles. There are single-parent Kwanzaas, extended-family Kwanzaas, neighborhood Kwanzaas, community Kwanzaas, and even workplace Kwanzaas. For more than a decade I was the mistress of ceremonies at a Kwanzaa celebration hosted by the Africana Studies department at Queens College/CUNY in New York City, where I taught. Each year the celebration grew and offered the Black faculty and staff a chance to get together and remind the institution and themselves of their presence and importance at the institution. Each Kwanzaa celebration brings something else to the kaleidoscope of possibilities that is the holiday.

While the basic Nguzo Saba (Seven Principles) remain unchanged, celebrants are open to find the way to the holiday that best expresses their individuality. Some followers of Kwanzaa fast from sunrise to sunset during the seven days, as with the Muslim Ramadan. Needless to say, this makes the gathering for the evening meal more celebratory. Others invite different friends in to celebrate throughout the seven days, or have gatherings to remind the children of the family of the seven principles. Still others celebrate Kwanzaa without even knowing that they're doing it. All of those New Year's Eve gatherings and New Year's Day open houses can fall right into the category of the Kwanzaa gatherings, whatever they're called. All that are missing are the *mazao*, and the *mkeka*, the *kinara* with the *mishumaa saba*, the *muhindi*, the *kikombe cha umoja*, and the *zawadi*. Once I realized that about my own holidays, I easily incorporated the symbols into the festivities along with the New World Yoruba feeding of the ancestors that was already included.

The Kwanzaa that you will find between these covers is my personal Kwanzaa: an individual riff that can be embroidered on at your whim to create *your* Kwanzaa. My aunt Clara always used to say, "You don't have a holiday, you have to *make* a holiday." In this she spoke the truth. The personal meaning of each and every holiday comes from the manner and commitment with which the celebrants choose to participate in it.

My Kwanzaa is informed by two main factors in my life: family and ritual. My family has always been the nucleus of my being. Pride in my parents, their accomplishments, their perseverance, their ability to survive in a world that was not always kind, and my desire to live up to their standards have been strong motivating factors.

I am also an individual steeped in a love of history and tradition. As a retired teacher and culinary historian, I believe it is important that we know about our past. As an internationalist, I believe it is important that we know about the cultures of peoples of African descent around the globe. As a spiritual being, I believe it is important that we honor those who went before so that we build on their deeds in creating our own future.

In 1995, I was a relative newcomer to the holiday of Kwanzaa, but when I looked at the holiday, I realized that I'd been celebrating it all of my adult life in my own personal way. I may have been out of sync, but I was always in the spirit. My personal celebration has usually taken place on only one of the days of the holiday: January 1. On that day for more than twenty years, I opened my home to friends old and new, to relatives, and to new acquaintances whose spirits spoke to me. Over the years that it was held, the gathering grew from a few friends who were invited over to meet my parents to a gathering of fifty or more individuals from around the world.

At one celebration, Haitians, Brazilians, Senegalese, Guyanese, Ethiopians, and Americans of all hues gathered to start the year. A Muslim religious leader shared conversation with a Yoruba priestess, while a precocious eleven-year-old offered his views on polygamy to an astonished group of single over-forty women. My eighty-one-year-old mother danced a few vigorous steps to some Zairian *soukouss* music, while my Uncle Herbie, who's really not my uncle but has known me all of my life, guarded the door. There was a heaping plate of food on the floor in the kitchen for my ancestors, who were called by name in a small New World Yoruba ceremony just prior to the serving of the food. There was music, food, drink, good times, reminiscence, reflection, and communion. In short, there was Kwanzaa.

The menu was selected to salute my Black American ancestry and my international life. Each year there's Hoppin' John for luck and collard greens for folding money. There's also roast pork for sheer colored cussedness, survival, and a universal desire to live high on the hog. A mixture of okra, corn, and tomatoes is served with hot chile to fire us up for the oncoming year and to remind us of our origins. For internationality, there's always a diaspora dish from Brazil, the Caribbean, or the Motherland, that changes annually.

The gathering has become so much a part of my celebration of the first of the year that for many decades my budget and my life were planned around it. My Kwanzaa continued until 2000, which was the year that my mother died. Following her death, I became a holiday orphan and often spent Christmases in New Orleans celebrating with friends there. I became a part of their community and left my New York Kwanzaa behind. Now, with young friends having children and with the world roiling in turmoil that calls for Black Americans to come together as a people to seriously think of new ways and real solutions to twenty-first-century issues, I feel that a return to Kwanzaa is again essential.

As I look around at the Black American community, I find that I have unwittingly allowed myself some leeway because I do not have children. However, the responsibilities of Kwanzaa go beyond the family to extended family and to the community, and there, we all have children. Our children need the sense of specialness that comes from participating in a known and loved ritual. They need the mastery of self-discipline that comes from order. They need the pride and self-awareness that comes from a knowledge of their past as well as the stability that comes from a holiday that offers continuity and hope. In brief, they need Kwanzaa as a tool for building their future and our own.

PREPARING FOR KWANZAA

Kwanzaa, whether it's your first or your fiftieth, is a joyous time of anticipation and festivity. The holiday takes on greater meaning if as much thought is put into the preparation as goes into the celebration. Begin by reading about the holiday and knowing what its original background and purpose were. The best source on that is the work by the man who created the holiday: Dr. Maulana Karenga. Some have issues with Karenga's personal history, and others are skeptical about the Black Nationalist origins of the holiday. However, no home that celebrates the holiday should be without a copy of either *Kwanzaa Origin, Concepts, and Practice* (Kawaida, 1975) or *The Black American Holiday of Kwanzaa: A Celebration of Family, Community & Culture* (University of Sankore Press, 1989). Several other works offer personal explanations of the holiday and suggestions for celebrating it; check with your local bookstore and online. (This is a good time to practice the principle of Ujamaa, cooperative economics; think of independent Black American bookstores first.) Think also of local organizations in your town or city that may have communal celebrations of Kwanzaa in which you and your family may wish to participate.

After you have decided just how you wish to celebrate the holiday, be sure that you have the Seven Basic Symbols of Kwanzaa:

- The *mazao*, the fruit and vegetables that represent the roots of the celebration as a harvest ceremony, you can obtain from your greengrocer. (Again, think Ujamaa.) Look to those fruits and vegetables emblematic of the African diaspora. Think of okra and black-eyed peas, of true yams and watermelons. Then, add some New World fruits and vegetables like pumpkins and squashes, sweet potatoes and pineapples. Think of all the bounty of the Motherland and of this hemisphere that we eat daily. A proverb states, "Before eating, thank the food." In your creation of your Kwanzaa arrangement of *mazao*, think of the fruits and vegetables that have enabled us to survive on both sides of the Atlantic. A horn of plenty or cornucopia is inappropriate as it harks back to European traditions. You may, therefore, wish to use African or Black American baskets or bowls in organizing your Kwanzaa display. Think of the sweetgrass baskets of Senegal or the Low Country Gullah baskets that are their New World iteration. Consider the intricately woven baskets of Kenya, or the incised calabash gourds of Benin, or carved wooden bowls from Haiti, or red heart trays from Guyana. As you set up the display, thank the fruits and vegetables for contributing to our survival.

- The *mkeka*, the mat, holds the display together and symbolizes the foundation of the holiday and our foundations as a people. A proverb states, "If you know who you are, you know where you're going." Select a piece of fabric from the African diaspora to serve as your placemat, but not just because it's pretty. Select it because you know what it is, where it's from, and why you have chosen it. Ghana's *kente* has become a symbol of the Motherland for many of us, but there are other possibilities. Try a piece of Kenya's *kitenge* or Nigeria's *aso oke*. A tie-dyed fabric from the Côte d'Ivoire or an austere piece of Malian mudcloth, or an intricate piece of Kasai velvet from Zaire, or even a mat handcrocheted by a family elder could all serve. You may even choose to make your own (see Family Mkeka, page 64).

- The *kinara*, the candleholder, symbolizes our ancestors and it should be chosen with care, or constructed with love, to honor them. In early Kwanzaa celebrations, the *kinara* was used to symbolize *nkulunkulu*, the firstborn, the one who is at the beginning of our people and our principles. First-time celebrants should be reminded that a *kinara* is not a Jewish menorah. (A *kinara* has seven branches while a menorah has nine.) The *kinara*'s seven candles, or *mishumaa*, are placed with the black candle in the middle, the red candles to the left, and the green candles to the right. Following the first day of Kwanzaa, on which the black central candle is lighted, the candles are lighted alternately from left to right, reinforcing visually the image that without struggle (represented by the red candles), there is no future (represented by the green ones).

- The *muhindi*, the ears of corn, represent the number of children in each household. They signify continuity and potential as corn grows from corn and each ear has the potential within it of becoming a stalk and, in turn, producing other ears. Children represent our continuity and here they are celebrated. Even if there are no children in the family, one ear is placed to acknowledge that we are all responsible for our children.

- The *kikombe cha umoja*, the communal cup of unity, symbolizes the unity of all peoples of African descent. It is used to pour *tambiko*, the libation, to the four cardinal points in the honor of the ancestors and is also passed among the celebrants of the holiday as a sign of solidarity. Select a communal cup that speaks culturally to the holiday. It may be a simple gourd or a richly carved wooden chalice.

- The *zawadi*, gifts, are also a part of the holiday celebration. They may be given throughout the holiday or on a particular night to celebrate a special victory with that principle. The *zawadi* of Kwanzaa are not given automatically, but rather given as rewards for promises kept, tasks accomplished, difficulties overcome, and progress made. In selecting Kwanzaa *zawadi*, emphasis should be placed on education and cultural value. Books make excellent gifts, particularly those by African, Black

American, and African diaspora authors, and those that discuss aspects of our history and culture. Because Kwanzaa aims to avoid the commercialization that has overtaken the other year-end festivities, handmade gifts are also especially appropriate, whether made by the giver or by other Black Americans. Again, as with all Kwanzaa purchases, in buying Kwanzaa *zawadi*, the principle of Ujamaa should be kept in mind. With Kwanzaa symbols and handmade Kwanzaa gifts, the principle of Kuumba should be kept in the forefront.

For all of its serious principles, though, Kwanzaa is also a time of feasting, of rejoicing, of savoring friendships and ties with family, of renewing commitments. Part of that communion of family and friends takes place around the table, and the communion of the table is a good part of the warmth of the holiday. We as a people have for centuries communed in the kitchen. We have for generations gathered around scarred wooden tables shelling peas and picking pieces of meat off a chicken or turkey carcass. We've lifted lids off steaming pots of savory stews and slow-cooked vegetables and sampled tastes of what's cooking off the edges of wooden spoons. We have come together at thousands of wedding banquets, christening feasts, and family reunions. We have shared sorrows and mourned over funeral meats and casseroles of macaroni and cheese. We have danced with friends, grieved lost loves, advised children, and planned protests around kitchen tables. During the holiday of Kwanzaa, we again come together in our own personal kitchen communion, using the table as a locus for reaffirming our family values, our personhood, and our principles as a people. The recipes in this book are designed so that all family members, whatever their ages and abilities, can participate in their creation.

There are also projects for each night, designed to bring the family together. The projects are simple and can be done by tiny fingers with blunt-edged scissors, or by gnarled hands that are too bent to hold a needle. They are for all the family members. Some work to help the community; some celebrate the family and provide a record of growth; some provide continuity and highlight Kuumba, creating Kwanzaa symbols for use in future years.

Finally, there are blank pages throughout the book so that family members can add their own recipes, reminiscences, and history, and create a personal work for each family that will truly be a Kwanzaa keepsake.

Use the book as a building block for your family's Kwanzaa memories, fill it with recipes, photographs, family history, and lore. Write in the margins, fold down the pages at favorite dishes, paste in recipes snipped from other sources. Keep family birthdates and history in between its covers and transform it into a talisman and keepsake for future generations. Kwanzaa is about unity. Never is a family or a group more together than when it sits down to table. During the holiday of Kwanzaa, use the pages of this book and the table-time communion of the holiday to heal old wounds, build new bridges, forge new friendships, and create new futures for your family and for all of our families.

THE GRIOT'S PAGES

African writer Amadou Hampâté Bâ said that on that continent, "when an elder dies a library burns down."

The Christian Bible says, "In the beginning was the Word." Africans and people of African descent throughout the world understand this only too well. We are a people of the word: juking and jiving, talking and testifying, speechifying and signifying, preaching and teaching. Our griots are true masters of the word, savoring each nuance of language and meaning with a delight that is contagious. Think of the sermons of unknown ministers, the pyrotechnical word-smithing of rappers, and the songs of the minstrels of Mali. Formerly, our griots were unknown bards, troubadours armed with koras and harps, drums and cymbals recalling the deeds of heroes like Sundiata of Mali and Chaka of the Zulu. Today, they capture our ephemeral words from the air and place them on paper for the future. Their names are known. They are called Maryse Condé and Maya Angelou, Ismael Reed and Imamu Baraka, Nicolas Guillen and Wole Soyinka, Samuel Selvon and Toni Morrison, Chinua Achebe and "Miss Lou" Bennett, Langston Hughes and Paul Lawrence Dunbar, Zora Neale Hurston, Gwendolyn Brooks, James Baldwin, Henry Louis Gates, Jesamyn Ward, Imani Perry, Isabel Wilkerson, Rita Dove, Natasha Trethewey, Tracy Smith, Amanda Gorman, and more, oh, so many, many more.

Each family has its own griot as well, the one who knows the birthdays and the telephone numbers, where the great-aunts are and where great-grandaddy really came from. As this holiday of Kwanzaa will celebrate the ancestors of your family, these pages are where the family griot can record your family history. Write the names and birthdays of all of the members of your immediate lineage that you know: mother/father, grandmother/grandfather on each side, and so forth as far back as possible. Many have used companies like ancestry.com, 23andMe.com, and various sources using DNA to take families on a deep dive into their origins and background. These pages are where to begin to make that information a part of the ongoing family record.

FAMILY PAGES

JESSICA B. HARRIS

FAMILY PAGES

FAMILY PAGES

JESSICA B. HARRIS

FAMILY PAGES

....

....

....

....

....

....

....

....

....

....

....

....

....

....

....

....

FAMILY PAGES

....

....

....

....

....

....

....

....

....

....

....

....

....

....

....

....

....

....

THE FIRST NIGHT

UMOJA

(UNITY)

strive for and maintain unity in the family, community, nation, and race

When spider webs unite, they can tie up a lion.
—Ethiopian proverb

On the first night of the holiday, as on all nights of the holiday, the celebration begins with the asking of the question *Habari gani?* (What's the news?) The answer is the principle of the day. As this is the first day of the holiday, the response is Umoja. The lighting of one of the seven candles on the *kinara* and the pouring of the libation from the *kikombe cha umoja* follow the asking of the question. On this, the first day of the holiday, the black candle at the center of the *kinara* is lighted. As the candle is lighted, the person lighting the candle should discuss what the principle of Umoja means. After the candle is lighted, *tambiko* (libation) is poured to the four cardinal points of the globe. (The pouring of the libation may accompany the saluting of the ancestors with a name called for each of the cardinal points of the compass.) Finally, the communal cup is passed around and the celebrants should sip from it. (If health concerns make sharing a cup inadvisable, pouring the libation can suffice.) While *tambiko* is poured, or as the cup is passed, the ancestors are saluted.

Tonight is the night we celebrate the spirit of Umoja (unity).

Tonight, and all nights of the year, we celebrate the spirits of those who have gone before, who represent the values of Umoja.

We celebrate the spirits of:
Kwame Nkrumah of Ghana
Mae Aninha of Ile Axe Opo Afonja in Brazil
Marcus Garvey of Jamaica
Mary McLeod Bethune of the United States
Simon Nkoli of South Africa
_____ (your family selection[s])

and the spirits of all others who have gone before who understood the need to maintain unty in our families, in our communities, nations, and in our race. We celebrate the spirits of all of those who understood that all children of Mother Africa around the globe are unified and share a common heritage and a common destiny.

Tonight, and all nights, we celebrate the spirits of all of those who are here with us now.

Tonight, and all nights, we celebrate the spirits of those who are yet to come.

Following the saluting of the ancestors, there should be a few minutes' conversation about their lives and accomplishments. The brief biographies here are simply springboards to discussion. Each family should add and subtract names from the list as they please in the space provided. In each case, though, all present should know why the spirit has been selected. In this book, I have selected to salute the spirits of those who have gone on to become the ancestor-spirits of the African-Atlantic world. I have made an effort to select those who are not as well known as some of our other ancestor spirits. I have passed over Malcolm, Martin, and Frederick Douglass in favor of Kwame Nkrumah, Mae Aninha, Marcus Garvey, Mary McLeod Bethune, Fannie Lou Hamer, and Zumbi, among others, in an effort to widen our horizons and push us all beyond the boundaries of our own cultures. For this edition, I have added special biographies saluting our LGBTQ+ ancestors from across the diaspora as well, to remind us all to always honor our entire community; for when we recognize one another across the divides of language, sexual orientation, gender, religion, culture, and geography, we are all richer for it. These biographies, though, are only the first step. Your family may wish to include those who still walk among us and even members of your own family who represent the evening's particular Nguzo Saba. Add your biographies; follow the principle of Kuumba, creativity, in your own celebration.

KWAME NKRUMAH OF GHANA
(1909–1972)

Born in Nkroful in the Western Province of the British Gold Coast (now Ghana) in 1909, Kwame Nkrumah was the son of a goldsmith. In the traditions of his people, he was named Kwame because he was born on a Saturday. Nkrumah was educated in colonial schools and trained as a teacher at Achimota College. He taught for five years and then journeyed to the United States, where he enrolled at Lincoln University, an HBCU in Pennsylvania. He attended Lincoln for seven years, receiving bachelor of arts and bachelor of theology degrees. At the same time, he also attended the University of Pennsylvania and received master of science and master of arts degrees. Nkrumah financed his schooling by working as an unskilled laborer.

Upon completion of his schooling, Nkrumah went to England and became active in anticolonialist Pan-African politics. He was invited to return to Ghana as the secretary of the Gold Coast Convention in 1947. For nine years, Nkrumah fought for the independence of his country. On March 6, 1957, Nkrumah became the prime minister of a state that was renamed Ghana in honor of the ancient African empire. Ghana was the first Sub-Saharan African country to gain its independence from colonial rule. In 1960, a republic was declared, and Nkrumah became Ghana's first elected president. Political upheavals followed and Nkrumah was overthrown by a coup in 1966. He died in exile in 1972. His remains were eventually entombed in a mausoleum in Accra that has been restored and was re-opened to the public in 2023.

We salute Kwame Nkrumah tonight because he was one of the founding fathers of contemporary Africa. We salute the spirit of Kwame Nkrumah tonight because as one of the founding fathers of Pan-Africanism, he left us the task of attaining the unity of all peoples of African descent throughout the world.

MAE ANINHA (EUGENIA ANNA DOS SANTOS) OF BRAZIL (1869–1938)

Born July 13, 1869, Eugenia Anna dos Santos lived in a Brazil where slavery was still legal. (It would only be abolished finally in that country in 1888.) The daughter of two members of the Gurunsi nation who had been enslaved in the city of Salvador da Bahia de Todos os Santos (Bahia), Brazil, she grew up knowing firsthand the poverty and the despair of slavery in the hemisphere. As a youngster, she was initiated into the religion of her ancestors, a religion that celebrated venerated ancestors and the African forces of nature called *orixas* in the Yoruba language as spoken in Brazil. She was initiated as a votary of the *orixa* Xango Ogodo and Afonja. Her initiation name in the Yoruba of her ancestors was Oba Biyi, which signaled her devotion to Xango. She studied with her elders and was invited to become a part of the Candomblé community of Ile Iya Nasso Oka, Engenho Velho, better known as Casa Branca. However, following a disagreement over ritual matters, Mae Aninha left the Candomblé and founded her own house.

Later she would purchase land in São Gonçalo do Retiro, then on the outskirts of town, where she would establish her own religious community under the name of Ile Axe Opo Afonja. This community, like Casa Branca from which it sprang and numerous others throughout Brazil, is a living witness to the continuity of African values in the hemisphere. Mae Aninha and others like her throughout the hemisphere maintained their unity with Africa in their spiritual practices, saluting the gods of their ancestors and the *orixas* of their forbears; these New World keepers of Mother Africa's spiritual flames are also links in our chain of unity. Neither politician nor Pan-Africanist, Mae Aninha of Brazil also embodied the virtues of unity.

We salute the spirit of Eugenia Anna dos Santos (Mae Aninha) tonight as one who was a link in the golden chain that binds us eternally to the continent of our ancestors. We salute her personal vision of the spiritual unity of Africa and the Americas, one that gives us a view to the future while remembering the past.

MARCUS GARVEY OF JAMAICA
(1887–1940)

Born at Saint Ann's Bay, Jamaica, on August 17, 1887, Marcus Mosiah Garvey Jr. spent his youth as an apprentice printer learning firsthand what it meant to be poor and Black in colonial Jamaica. Later, while working as a printer, he crystallized the ideas that would lead him to found a small organization with a big name and an even bigger impact: The United Negro Improvement Association (UNIA). The organization was dedicated to the idea that political, military, and economic independence was the only way that the New World's peoples of African origin could uplift themselves. Garvey called for self-reliance for Africans, "at home and abroad."

By 1916, Jamaica had become too small a forum for his then radical ideas, and Garvey, after traveling in Central and South America, settled in New York City's Harlem, where he founded another branch of the UNIA. He began to speak of a "Back to Africa" movement. The UNIA grew in size as discussion of repatriation to Africa became a watchword for many Black Americans. With contributions from interested people, Garvey established a newspaper, *Negro World*, opened branches of the UNIA throughout the country, and even formed the Black Star Line, a steamship company designed to transport descendants back to Africa. It was not to be. Garvey's negotiations with the state of Liberia fell through, and conflicts with Black American leaders and legal and financial difficulties ensued. Garvey's troubles culminated in his being jailed for mail fraud in 1922. His sentence was commuted and he was deported to Jamaica in 1927 and died in London in 1940.

We salute the spirit of Marcus Mosiah Garvey tonight because he dared to dream of self-reliance and the unity of all Africans at home and abroad. We salute him because he took steps to fulfill that dream and because he left us his dream to attain.

MARY MCLEOD BETHUNE OF THE UNITED STATES (1875–1955)

Born near the cotton fields of Mayesville, South Carolina, Mary McLeod Bethune was one of seventeen children born to formerly enslaved parents. Her parents instilled in her a lifelong love for education by selecting her as the only one of their children to be sent to school. It was felt that she would, in turn, teach her sisters and brothers. She attended local schools and then Scotia College in North Carolina and Moody Bible Institute in Chicago. She honored her promise and taught her siblings. She so took to teaching that, as a young woman, she moved to Daytona, Florida, and founded her own school for Black American women with $1.50 in cash, five students, and a rented cottage. She drilled her students in basic academics and religion and insisted on giving them skills that would enable them to find work once they left. By 1923 the school numbered a student body of three hundred and had a staff of twenty-five. It would ultimately become Bethune-Cookman College and is today Bethune Cookman University.

Mary McLeod Bethune was an active clubwoman with a particular interest in giving Black American women a voice. To that end, she founded the National Council of Negro Women in 1935 and served as the organization's president until 1949. An adviser to presidents, Bethune directed the Division of Negro Affairs of the National Youth Administration during Franklin Delano Roosevelt's New Deal. As the first Black American woman to head a federal office, she was a force in FDR's Washington, working to remind leaders of the Black American political presence.

We salute the spirit of Mary McLeod Bethune tonight because she taught us the virtues of dreaming and of making those dreams become reality.

We salute her tonight, for although she had attained much, she did not rest on her laurels. Instead, she reached back in her family and beyond her family to her community and her race to bring people together under the banner of unity. We salute her tonight because she said, "Look at me. I am black. I am beautiful."

SIMON NKOLI OF SOUTH AFRICA
(1957–1998)

Simon Nkoli was born into a Sesotho-speaking family in the Black Johannesburg township of Soweto, South Africa, during the period of apartheid. The conditions in his country led him to become an activist at a young age, and he joined the Congress of South African Students rising to position of secretary for the Transvaal division of the group.

Nkoli, though, was fighting his battles on two fronts and in 1983 joined the mainly white Gay Association of South Africa that maintained that it was apolitical and refused to support his race-related activism. His growing discontent with the association led him to form the Saturday Group, the first Black gay activist group in Africa.

Nkoli's activism led to his being arrested and faced with the death penalty. He was acquitted of charges and released from prison in 1988 and subsequently founded GLOW, the Gay and Lesbian Organization of the Witwatersrand with LGBTQ+ activist Beverley Palesa Ditsie and organized the first pride parade in South Africa, held in 1990. Nkoli was the first gay activist to meet with Nelson Mandela in 1994 and campaigned for the inclusion of protection from discrimination in the Bill of Rights of the 1994 South African Constitution. Nkoli, who was HIV positive and died of AIDS in 1998 in Johannesburg, was undeniably one of the African continent's first champions of LGBTQ+ rights.

We salute Simon Nkoli this evening for his unparalleled bravery in fighting for his and his community's rights. His life was a beacon that illuminated the shadows of discrimination and gave voice to the unrepresented. We salute Simon Nkoli for reminding all of us that all forms of oppression are linked and we are not free of one if the others remain.

The menu celebrating Umoja is a multinational supper highlighting the union of all peoples of African descent throughout the world, from Texas to Tunis, Savannah to Salvador da Bahia, and New York to Nigeria.

Appetizers
Seasoned Olives (page 28)
Pan-Roasted Almonds (page 29)

Salad
Fresh Greens with Avocado and Raspberries (page 30)

Main Dish
Méchoui-Style Leg of Lamb with Cumin, Mint, and Chile (page 32)

Condiment
Mint Nectarine Chutney (page 34)

Starch
Orzo with Slivered Almonds (page 36)

Dessert
Plain Cake with Drambuie Apricot Sauce (page 37)

Beverage
Classic Rum Punch (page 38)

SEASONED OLIVES

Serves 6 to 8

In Brazil, olives frequently appear on the table as appetizers to heighten the appetite before a meal. This is probably a part of the nation's Lusitanian heritage.

Here, they are given additional flavor and zest by adding herbs and spices to them. This is one version; you can also use your own favorite seasonings to create a variation that is all your own.

1 pound canned ripe olives, drained

1 tablespoon dried thyme

1 teaspoon minced garlic

1 teaspoon minced fresh habanero or other hot chile, or to taste

2 tablespoons extra virgin olive oil

Salt and freshly ground black pepper

Prick each olive several times with the point of a sharp knife or a fork and place them in a medium bowl. Add the thyme, garlic, chile, olive oil, and salt and pepper to taste and mix them together well with a wooden spoon, making sure that all of the seasonings are well distributed. Cover with plastic wrap and refrigerate overnight. Serve chilled.

The olives will keep for a week or so in the refrigerator, if they last that long.

PAN-ROASTED ALMONDS

Serves 6

Driving into the Ourika Valley outside of Marrakesh, Morocco, one may be stopped along the way by small boys selling geodes. When these dull rocks are broken open, they reveal crystalline forms of amethyst and other brilliant delights. The same young boys also sell almonds, wonderful almonds that have a taste like those nowhere else on earth. The same almonds can be purchased, raw, roasted, or sugar-toasted, at the vendors' stalls in Marrakesh's Djema el Fna, the legendary square where jugglers and itinerant dentists, snake charmers, merchants, and magicians meet.

Almonds frequently turn up in the cooking of Morocco. Here, though, they're just blanched and then cooked to a golden brown for a before-dinner nibble.

2 cups skin-on almonds

2 tablespoons extra virgin olive oil

Salt (optional)

In a medium saucepan, bring at least 4 cups of water to a boil. Plunge the almonds into the boiling water and allow them to boil for 2 minutes.

Drain the almonds and, when slightly cooled, slip the brown skins from the almond kernels with your hands. Discard the skins and reserve the kernels.

In a heavy cast-iron skillet, heat 1 tablespoon of the olive oil over low heat. Add half of the almonds to the skillet and toast them in the oil, stirring occasionally, until they are golden brown, about 3 to 5 minutes. Drain them on paper towels. Repeat the process with the remaining 1 tablespoon olive oil and the other half of the almonds. Salt the almonds to taste, if desired, by placing them in a bag with some salt and shaking them until they are evenly coated. Serve warm.

The almonds will keep for a few weeks in the refrigerator, but they are better when prepared fresh, so make small batches.

FRESH GREENS WITH AVOCADO AND RASPBERRIES

Serves 6 to 8

Many people of African descent are meat-and-potato-eaters, preferring to get their vegetables in slow-cooked stews and sauces. With today's concerns about healthy eating, though, salads have come to the fore and in preparing them we use ingredients from around the world in testimony to the culinary internationality of the African diaspora.

This salad is a simple one of light fresh greens, tropical avocados, and the sweet surprise of forced winter raspberries. It's tossed with a light dressing prepared with a hint of sesame oil.

3 medium heads Boston lettuce
1 small sweet onion, cut crosswise
    into very thin slices
2 Hass avocados, cut into 1-inch
    cubes

½ cup fresh raspberries, rinsed and
    picked over
Light Soy–Sesame Dressing (recipe
    follows)

Discard the tough outer leaves of the lettuce. Rinse the rest of the leaves and pick over to remove brown spots and dirt. Tear the lettuce leaves into bite-size pieces. Pat the leaves dry on paper towels and place them in a large glass salad bowl.

Separate the onion slices into rings and add them to the salad bowl along with the avocado and raspberries. Pour the dressing over the salad, toss, and serve immediately.

LIGHT SOY-SESAME DRESSING

Makes a generous ¾ cup

The sugar is to cut the tartness of the vinegar, and you may find that you want a bit more or less depending on the type of rice vinegar you use.

⅓ cup reduced-sodium soy sauce

⅓ cup rice vinegar

2 tablespoons water

1 tablespoon sesame oil

¼ teaspoon brown sugar, or to taste

Salt and freshly ground black pepper

In a small bowl, whisk together the soy sauce, vinegar, water, sesame oil, brown sugar, and salt and pepper to taste until the ingredients are well mixed.

MÉCHOUI-STYLE LEG OF LAMB WITH CUMIN, MINT, AND CHILE

Serves 6 to 8

In Senegal, West Africa, in a small restaurant in Les Almadies called Chez M'Baye M'Barrik, I first tasted the dish called *méchoui*. This festive dish of spit-roasted lamb is traditional in much of the Maghreb and has made its way down to Senegal. At the restaurant, diners were presented with a whole roasted baby lamb and they picked off succulent bits to eat with their fingers. I've had variations of this wonderful dish in Senegal, in Tunisia, and in Morocco. In each place, the dish is slightly differently seasoned, as the tastes of the region, and indeed of the country, influence the flavors of the *méchoui*.

This is my personal variation on the *méchoui* theme. It uses a leg of lamb and a dry marinade combining the North African tastes of mint and cumin with the sub-Saharan African taste of chile. Leftovers can be used to make a quick dish of curried lamb.

1 shank end half leg of lamb (4 to 5 pounds)	1 tablespoon freshly ground black pepper
3 cloves garlic, slivered	1 tablespoon ground cumin
2 tablespoons extra virgin olive oil	2 tablespoons dried mint
1 tablespoon salt	⅛ teaspoon ground habanero chile or other hot chile powder, or to taste

Preheat the oven to 450°F.

Trim all excess fat and the fell from the lamb, then pierce the lamb skin with 15 or so small incisions. Insert the garlic slivers into the slits. Slather the olive oil over the lamb and rub it in with your hands. Place the salt, black pepper, cumin, mint, and chile in a spice grinder and pulse until they are well mixed. Then pat the dry rub over the lamb, covering the entire leg well. Place the lamb on a rack in a roasting pan.

Place the lamb in the oven and roast for 15 minutes. Then reduce the oven temperature to 350°F and continue to roast the lamb until the internal temperature registers 140°F for rare, 150°F for medium, or 160°F for well done on a meat thermometer, about 1 additional hour. (Cooking times will vary according to the shape of the lamb and the heat of your oven.)

Allow the meat to rest at room temperature for 20 minutes, then carve the leg of lamb parallel to the bone in long thin slices and serve.

MINT NECTARINE CHUTNEY

Makes about 2 cups

When I was a child, roast lamb was never served without the accompanying mint jelly. The combination of the coolness of the mint and the taste of the lamb was just perfect.

Today the habit of eating spicy condiments with roasted meats is alive and well in the African-Atlantic world. The mint jelly of my childhood has given way to numerous condiments, some fiery hot, some spicy. This chutney is one that I have been playing around with since 1985, when I wrote a book about peppers and chiles around the world called *Hot Stuff*. In this version the freshness of the mint is highlighted with the taste of nectarines and given a bit of kick with hot chile.

1 bunch fresh mint (about ten 3-inch-long sprigs)	1-inch piece fresh ginger, scraped
3 large firm nectarines, peeled and coarsely chopped	2 cloves garlic, peeled but whole
¼ teaspoon minced fresh habanero or other hot chile, or to taste	1 small onion, coarsely chopped
	½ cup cider vinegar
	½ cup sugar

Pull the mint leaves off the tough stems and place the leaves in a food processor (discard the stems). Add the nectarines, chile, ginger, garlic, and onion and pulse until you have a thick paste. (You may have to drizzle in a bit of the vinegar to get the mixture going.) Continue to pulse until all of the ingredients are pulverized.

Place the paste in a nonreactive medium saucepan and add the remaining vinegar and the sugar, stirring them in well to make sure that they are evenly mixed. Set the saucepan over heat and bring it slowly to a boil. Reduce the heat and simmer, stirring occasionally, until the chutney has thickened and taken on a jamlike consistency, about 30 minutes. Be careful not to let the bottom of the chutney burn or stick to the saucepan during the final minutes of cooking.

When the chutney is ready, spoon it into sterilized glass jars, allow it to cool, and refrigerate it until it is to be served. The chutney is particularly good with lamb, but will go well with any roasted or grilled meat. It will keep in the refrigerator for 4 to 6 days or make a larger batch and preserve it using traditional canning methods.

ORZO WITH SLIVERED ALMONDS

Serves 6 to 8

Cooking rice is a fine art. While it would seem simple to many, it is all too easy to transform the delicate dish into a coagulated glob of white paste. With this in mind, I sometimes cheat by using orzo, the rice-shaped pasta, in place of white rice. In this case, I jazz up the orzo with the addition of some slivers of almonds and a dash of orange flower water. (You can keep a few pan-roasted almonds back from the hungry hordes after you've prepared the appetizer.)

1 tablespoon extra virgin olive oil
1 pound orzo
¼ cup Pan-Roasted Almonds
   (page 29), slivered

½ teaspoon orange flower water
   (optional)
Orange segments, for garnish
Chopped parsley, for garnish

In a large saucepan, bring about 5 quarts of water and the olive oil to a boil. Add the orzo and cook for 7 minutes. Add the slivered almonds and continue to cook until the orzo is completely cooked, about 3 minutes. Drain the orzo and, if you choose, sprinkle it with the orange flower water. Serve hot, garnished with orange segments and parsley.

PLAIN CAKE WITH DRAMBUIE APRICOT SAUCE

Serves 6 to 8

I am not a dessert eater by nature. In fact, it was only a few years ago that I noticed that visitors to my home were not terribly happy when at the end of the meal I happily presented them with a good cup of coffee and a fresh fruit salad. I've learned my lesson and have been truly humbled.

The Black American way with sweets is serious. Folks want dessert! I'm still not a dessert fan, but I've learned a whole bagful of tricks that will produce a dessert to make any sugar freak smile with delight. This thick apricot-based sauce redolent of Drambuie is one of them. It's excellent when served with a plain yellow cake.

1 cup dried apricots
⅔ cup apricot preserves
2 tablespoons apricot
  nectar

2 tablespoons Drambuie liqueur,
  or to taste
1 teaspoon fresh lemon juice
6 to 8 servings plain yellow cake
  (see Note)

In a saucepan, combine the dried apricots with water to cover, Bring to a boil over high heat. Then reduce the heat and simmer the apricots until they are plumped, about 10 minutes. Drain the apricots. When cool enough to handle, snip them into small pieces with kitchen shears and set aside.

In a food processor, combine the apricot preserves, apricot nectar, Drambuie, and lemon juice and pulse until you have a thick syrup.

Pour the syrup into a bowl, add the snipped apricots, and stir them in so that each piece is well coated with the liquid.

The sauce can be refrigerated for 30 minutes and served chilled, or it can be placed in a saucepan and warmed. Either way, just drizzle it over the slices of cake. It transforms plain cake into something special.

Note: You can make your cake from scratch or from a doctored-up mix, or you can buy one from the local bakery.

CLASSIC RUM PUNCH

Rum is the classic beverage of the Caribbean. No self-respecting Guyanese, Haitian, Jamaican, or Trinidadian party would ever think of beginning a celebration without at least one bottle of rum on the table. Rum is a part of those of us who were enslaved on those shores to work the cane.

In much of the Caribbean, the first rum out of the bottle is traditionally poured on the ground for the ancestors. A Caribbean friend of mine tells tales of how her mother despaired of ever having a living room rug because her father insisted that the area around his chair be free from encumbrances so that he could pour his rum onto the floor. It is only fitting that on the first night of Kwanzaa, those who partake of alcohol celebrate unity with those from the Caribbean region with a glass of rum.

You may use the first pouring of your bottle tonight in the *kikombe cha umoja* to salute the spirits of all of those who went before, whether from the Caribbean region or not. With the rest, why not prepare a classic rum punch? The popular saying goes:

> *One of sour*
> *Two of sweet*
> *Three of strong*
> *Four of weak*

The "sour" is freshly squeezed lime juice. The "sweet" is sugar or sugar syrup. The "strong" is the rum. (Purchase the best you can afford; yes, there is a difference! I prefer the Rhum Agricole from the French islands that is prepared from sugarcane juice and not from molasses.) The "weak" is water to round it off. Whether for a single drink or a vat, the one, two, three, four system will keep you on the right track. Drink moderately: It goes down easy but it packs a true kick!

PROJECT: FAMILY COOKBOOK

ONE OF THE AIMS of Kwanzaa is to bring together families and friends in productive ways. To this end, each night will conclude with a project. The project can be done on the night or it can be done at any time during the holiday or the year to culminate in a Kwanzaa gift for the following year.

On the first night of Kwanzaa, Umoja, or unity, is saluted with the creation of a cookbook of family favorites. Most of us know only too well that we rarely ask for the recipe for something until it is too late. When grandma's gone, we wish we knew how to make her beaten biscuits. When Aunt Dorcas moves away, we wish we had watched exactly how she fluted the edges of her pies.

Begin this first night of Kwanzaa by making a conscious effort to write down the favorite recipes of your family. Have each family member select a favorite recipe to work on. Start by using the blank pages in this book. Then, collect the recipes on sheets of paper to be kept in a file folder or a blank book. Add to the collection throughout the year as holidays and birthdays and special family times bring new recipes to mind. At the end of the year, remember that self-publishing is astonishingly easy. Online sources now allow you to make professional-looking books complete with photos of individuals and finished dishes. You can have copies made to present to other family members: a child going away to college, those leaving for another town. Alternatively, you can go old school and head to your local office supply shop and cut and paste and photocopy away. No matter which method you use, the result is sure to delight and will help to keep the family together and preserve your traditions for another generation.

FAMILY PAGES

JESSICA B. HARRIS

FAMILY PAGES

....

....

....

....

....

....

....

....

....

....

....

....

....

....

....

....

....

THE SECOND NIGHT

KUJICHAGULIA
(SELF-DETERMINATION)

to define ourselves, name ourselves,
create for ourselves, speak for ourselves
instead of being defined, named, created for,
and spoken for by others

Nobody will think you're somebody if you don't think so yourself.
—Traditional Black American saying

On the second night of the holiday, as on all nights of the holiday, the celebration begins with the pouring of the libation from the *kikombe cha umoja* and the lighting of one of the seven candles of the *kinara*. Tonight, the central black candle of Umoja and the first of the red candles on the left of the *kinara*, the candle of Kujichagulia, self-determination, are lighted. After the candles are lighted, the libation is poured or the *kikombe cha umoja* is passed around and thoughts turn to the spirits of those who represented the virtues of Kujichagulia in our society.

Tonight is the night we celebrate the spirit of Kujichagulia (self-determination).

Tonight, and all nights of the year, we celebrate the spirits of those who have gone before who represent the values of Kujichagulia.

We celebrate the spirits of:
    Chaka Zulu of South Africa
    Zumbi of Palmares in Brazil
    Nanny of the Maroons in Jamaica
    Cinque of the Amistad *in the United States*
    Gladys Bentley of the United Sates
              _____ (your family selection[s])

and the spirits of all others who fought and died defining themselves, determining their destinies, and forging their futures and our own.

Tonight, and all nights, we celebrate the spirits of all those who are here with us.

Tonight, and all nights, we celebrate the spirits of those who are yet to come.

CHAKA ZULU OF SOUTH AFRICA
(NINETEENTH CENTURY)

Born the son of Nandi and Sanza'ngakona, in southern Africa in the first half of the nineteenth century, Chaka was a solitary child. His father was a leader of one of the clans of the Abatetwa, but because questions were raised about his legitimacy, Chaka spent much of his childhood treated as illegitimate and as an outcast. These hardships, though, only served to form the man that Chaka would become. He grew into a man of impressive physical strength and soon became a *mampoli*, or chieftain, to whom remarkable deeds were attributed. His actions only increased the jealousy of his half-brothers.

His life threatened, Chaka found refuge with his father's sovereign, Dinguiswayo, and became his trusted adviser and spokesman. He rapidly rose in the ranks, and on the death of his father recouped his rightful inheritance and became chief of his clan. His military valor became known, and in the political instability that followed the defeat and death of Dinguiswayo, he became the head of the majority of the Ngouni people. He celebrated his sovereignty by changing their name to one that sounded like the drums of wars or the thunders of the heavens: *Zulu* (which means "sky") or *Amazulus* (meaning "people from the sky"). He cemented his reign by reorganizing the armies into a military machine where training, strategy, and discipline were the watchwords. The army was divided into regiments of about a thousand individuals of about the same age. No detail was too small for Chaka's scrutiny. Sandals were eliminated because they slowed the warriors down; the throwing lance was eliminated in favor of the *assegai*, a spear or javelin, which encouraged close offensive hand-to-hand combat.

Chaka and his armies, with their new military might and their formidable strategy, overran southern Africa like a juggernaut. Chaka was a military man and constant war was the order of his empire. The circumstances surrounding his death are unknown, but it seems likely that he was assassinated in a political plot instigated by his half-brothers. His legendary final words reminded his murderers that they would not rule for long, for the whites were coming to drive them out. Now, his descendants and other Black South Africans have returned to power in the land that is theirs.

We salute Chaka tonight as a man who made his mark on history, one who united a dispersed people and moved them on to glory. We salute his skill in determining his own destiny and that of his people.

ZUMBI OF PALMARES IN BRAZIL
(SEVENTEENTH CENTURY)

Born within the precincts of the Northeastern Brazilian state of Pernambuco in 1655, Zumbi was unlike other Blacks born in Brazil in that period, who were automatically doomed to lives of enslavement. He was different; he was special; he was free! Zumbi was free because he was born within the stockaded walls of the legendary, but oh, so real, *quilombo* or Maroon settlement of former slaves, known as Palmares. Palmares, a name that still resonates in Brazil today, was a settlement established by runaway slaves; it grew to a community of several thousand people and lasted in the mountains of Pernambuco for more than fifty years.

Zumbi was born in Palmares, but as a baby, he was captured in one of the periodic European raids on the *quilombo*. He was given as a present to a priest in Porto Calvo who raised him and named him Francisco. The priest educated the small Black boy, teaching him Latin, Portuguese, and Catholicism, but he could not rid him of the taste of freedom on his tongue.

In 1670, Francisco ran away and returned to the mountains and the Palmares of his birth. The Palmares to which he returned was a loosely knit confederation of villages covering six thousand square kilometers, all under the rule of Ganga Zumba. At its height in 1672, Ganga Zumba's reign slipped into decline by 1680, when Zumbi assumed the mantle of leadership and prepared for war. He fortified parts of Palmares, surrounding strategic areas with stockades and palisades, and prepared to fight off the constant attacks from the European sugar lords of Pernambuco whose slaves looked to Palmares as salvation. The battles lasted for more than ten years, but finally, in January 1694, the final fight for Palmares began with a series of engagements equaled in size only by the Brazilian War of Independence 130 years later. The main part of Palmares fell on the sixth of February. For years, it was thought that Zumbi had died in a dramatic leap to his death off the edge of the abyss that made Palmares such a formidable fortress, but recent evidence suggests that he survived, along with about two thousand others, and continued to wage a guerrilla war against the colonial forces until November 1695, when he was betrayed and killed, leaving behind him the history of Palmares and a legacy of resistance to the domination of others.

We salute Zumbi of Palmares tonight because, born free, he worked, fought, and died to maintain that freedom and to ensure the freedom and self-determination of others.

NANNY OF THE MAROONS IN JAMAICA
(SEVENTEENTH AND EIGHTEENTH CENTURIES)

Where and when Nanny was born is lost in the whispering winds of history, but her importance to the people of Jamaica is written in tablets of stone. Whether she was born in Jamaica or in Africa is as unknown as the actual date of her birth, but it is thought that Nanny was the sister of Cudjoe, a renowned Jamaican rebel leader of the Maroons, who had their origins as escaped slaves of the Spaniards, and that she never personally experienced slavery. It is also thought that she had no children of her own, but that all of the people of her community became her children; she was the mother of her people in the traditional sense of the Akan Queen Mothers.

The community Nanny led was known as the Windward Maroons and had its capital at Nanny Town. It was thought to have been founded in the 1690s and consisted of over six hundred acres in the Back Rio Grande Valley in Portland, Jamaica. Much of the land was located on the northern slopes of the Blue Mountains. This community was ruled by Nanny when the town was "discovered" by the English in the 1730s. The English subsequently attempted to capture the town and re-enslave its residents. Fierce fighting between the English and Maroons broke out and continued throughout the years of the First Maroon Wars. Nanny dominated the Maroon fighting, not by actively participating herself, but rather by blessing the guerrilla fighters and directing the campaign strategy. Maroons fought by ambush, using stealth and their knowledge of the terrain to defeat their enemies. Nanny communicated with her forces via the Maroon *abeng*, a bugle carved from a cow horn, that could be heard throughout the mountain valleys and could be played so adeptly that the warriors could be summoned as though they were spoken to.

A priestess to her people, Nanny had powers beyond those of mere mortals: She was said to be able to catch bullets in her buttocks, rendering them harmless, and then return them; this power was called *nantucompong* in the Akan language that the Maroons retained from their African past. Foremost among the resistance leaders of her time, Nanny was determined never to cede to the English and made a trans-island trek with her people to avoid surrendering. She continued fighting until she reluctantly accepted peace terms by treaty in 1738. An unvanquished leader, she was granted a land parcel in Portland, Jamaica, by truce agreement in 1740 and continued to rule in peace until she died in the 1750s. She rests in Jamaican soil, a hero of the Jamaican nation, ever free and ever faithful to her ideals.

We salute Nanny of the Maroons tonight for her fierce, unswerving determination to guard the liberty of her people and to ensure that they and only they determined who they were.

CINQUE OF THE *AMISTAD* IN THE UNITED STATES
(EIGHTEENTH CENTURY)

No one is sure when the horrible journey began, but its second phase started in June 1839 when forty-nine men and four children newly arrived from the African coast were herded into the hold of a slave ship, ironically called the *Amistad* (Friendship), lying at anchor off the coast of Havana, Cuba. Many of the ship's captives were of the Mende people of Sierra Leone, among them Cinque, a twenty-five-year-old rice farmer and son of Mende nobles. The ship laden with captives for resale was bound for another part of Cuba, but it was not destined to arrive. The combination of a lax crew and a remarkably efficient group of Africans under the direction of Cinque resulted in one of history's most successful shipboard slave insurrections.

Overpowering the captain and cook, the men took control of the ship and ordered the Spaniards to sail them back to the West African coast, toward the rising sun. The Spaniards did so, but only by day, setting course by night for the northwest, where after a journey of two months they came into waters off the coast of Long Island. Cinque ordered anchor to be dropped and went ashore to attempt to secure provisions, but before the ship could set sail again, it was seized by an American naval vessel and taken to Connecticut. As mutineers, the captives were in danger of being extradited to Cuba to stand trial, a course favored by the Cuban and Spanish governments and then president Martin Van Buren, who wished to avoid a diplomatic incident. However, Spain had outlawed slave importation into its territories, including Cuba, in 1817, and so the captives were not legally slaves. The matter was to be determined by the American judicial system in a trial that lasted eighteen months, going all the way to the Supreme Court, where former president John Quincy Adams pleaded the captives' cause, winning the day. It was agreed that they had been illegally sold and were not slaves. They were free. However, there were no funds for repatriation. Abolitionists eventually raised the money to send the Africans home and thirty-five survivors of the original fifty-three returned to Africa, narrowly escaping the voracious jaws of New World slavery.

Tonight, we salute the spirit of Cinque and the spirits of all his fellow captives of the *Amistad*. Despite overwhelming odds, they fought to determine their destinies and succeeded. They lost their freedom, dreamed of recapturing it, fought for freedom, and attained it. Their faith and their accomplishments are beacons to us all.

GLADYS ALBERTA BENTLEY OF THE UNITED STATES (1907–1960)

Attempting to define the life of Gladys Bentley is like trying to pick up water in cupped hands: much is always lost. Born to a Black American man and his Trinidadian wife, Bentley always felt that she was rejected by her mother because she was not a boy. "She wouldn't even nurse me, and my grandmother had to raise me for six months on a bottle before they could persuade my mother to take care of her own baby." Bentley always chose to dress in men's clothing, a practice she adopted as a child when she preferred to wear her brothers' clothes. She grew to be a talented musician and went on to become a performer, honing her singing and piano-playing talents in the crucible that was the circuit of clandestine pop-up rent parties that came to define Harlem's underground nightlfe in the early part of the twentieth century.

By the late 1920s she was appearing as a cross-dressing performer. She also appeared in the Prohibition-fed Harlem of speakeasies and slumming where a stint at Harry Hansberry's Clam House, a well-known gay spot in "Jungle Alley," brought notoriety and fame. Her songs were often risqué double entendre ones that commented on subjects ranging from sexual longings to social issues. By the early 1930s she was at the top of the marquee at Park Avenue's famed Ubangi Club where she was backed up by a chorus line of drag queens. Outré to the maximum, formal men's eveningwear would become her trademark look; her souvenir photos show her in a top hat, white tie, and tails: her signature outfit. In her act, she played piano, and sang her own scatological and scandalous lyrics to popular tunes of the day in a deep, growling voice while flirting with women in the audience. She reveled in the blurring of gender lines and is reputed to have had liaisons with both women and men. Her performances drew Black, white, gay, and straight audiences: Langston Hughes, Carl Van Vechten, and others celebrated her and were rabid fans. Her performances skirted the edges of decency and legality and she often performed under threat of being closed down by the police. By the end of the 1930s, as the glory days of the Harlem Renaissance ended, she toured the country, made records, and eventually relocated to California.

The later years of Bentley's life become confusing; she was one of the flash points for new McCarthy-era laws and had to carry a permit to be able to perform in men's clothing. By the 1950s, Bentley began wearing dresses, became a minister, and penned at least one article on how she had "cured" her homosexuality. She kept performing albeit in smaller and smaller venues, recorded a few songs, married a man, and is later thought to have married a woman. She died of pneumonia in California in 1960, her chameleon-like existence undefined. Since then, because of her early performances, her unquestionable talent, and her audacious persona, Bentley has become a celebrated LGBTQ+ icon.

We salute Gladys Bentley for her steadfast and stalwart self. We salute her because despite the cultural conventions of her times and imposed norms of behavior, she allowed no one to define her. She defined herself and despite all odds remained herself. If that's not self-determination . . . what is?

*The meal celebrating the Nguzo Saba of Kujichagulia
is a menu inspired by Africa comprising a variety of dishes
from the Motherland that celebrate our African roots.*

Appetizer
South African Sweet Potato Fritters (page 56)

Salad
Moroccan-Style Grilled Pepper Salad (page 57)

Main Dish
Senegalese Chicken Yassa (page 58)

Starch
Plain White Rice (page 60)

Condiment
Piment Aimée (Aimée's Hot Sauce) (page 61)

Dessert
Caramelized Ripe Plantains (page 62)

Beverage
The Naa Naa Marocain (Moroccan Mint Tea) (page 63)

SOUTH AFRICAN SWEET POTATO FRITTERS

Serves 6 to 8

Throughout the African continent, frying in deep oil is a culinary art form. The making of fritters and snacks by frying tasty tidbits in various oils has crossed the Atlantic with Africa's children to become emblematic of African cooking in the Western Hemisphere as well. Dishes like New Orleans rice fritters or *calas*; the Caribbean's codfish fritters, whether they're called *bacalaitos* or *acras de morue*; and Brazil's ambrosial *acaraje* all hark back to this tradition.

The sweet potato fritters that begin this night's menu are a South African invention. They, like variations of this dish throughout the continent, combine the sweet potato, a New World tuber, with an African culinary technique. One of the tricks to great fritters is to use clean oil and to make sure that the oil is hot enough before beginning.

These fritters can be accompanied by a spicy hot sauce when served as an appetizer course. Alternatively, they can be lightly dusted with sugar and served as a dessert.

Peanut oil, for deep-frying

1 pound sweet potatoes, peeled

½ cup all-purpose flour

1 large egg, beaten

Salt and freshly ground black pepper

Pour 2 inches of oil into a heavy saucepan or deep-fryer and heat to 375°F.

Grate the sweet potatoes into a medium bowl, cover them with boiling water, and let them stand for 15 minutes. Drain off the water and slowly add the flour, beaten egg, and salt and pepper to taste, stirring to make sure that they are well mixed. You should have a thickish paste that will hold its shape when picked up in a tablespoon. If the mixture is too thick, add a bit of warm water. If it is too thin, add a bit more flour.

Drop the mixture, a few tablespoons at a time, into the hot oil and cook the fritters until they float to the surface, 3 to 5 minutes, turning them once to make sure that they are slightly browned on each side. Drain on absorbent paper and serve hot.

MOROCCAN-STYLE GRILLED PEPPER SALAD

Serves 6 to 8

Formal meals in Morocco are lengthy events. The guests, who are traditionally seated on banquettes around low circular tables, are regaled with the best the household has to offer. Frequently the first course is a selection of small plates of vegetable salads, which are eaten with crusty pieces of flat bread. This salad is a variation on the traditional Moroccan salad known as *salata felfel* (*felfel* means "pepper" in Arabic).

If you want to make this dish even more special for Kwanzaa, you can use red, green, and the deep eggplant-hued bell peppers that are almost black for a black, red, and green salad.

1 pound mixed bell peppers	¼ teaspoon finely minced fresh
3 tablespoons extra virgin	cilantro
olive oil	2 teaspoons finely chopped fresh
1 tablespoon fresh lemon juice	flat-leaf parsley
½ teaspoon ground cumin	Salt and freshly ground black pepper

Preheat the broiler.

Place the peppers on a rack under the broiler and grill them until they are charred black on the outside, turning them frequently. When they are charred, wrap them in paper towels and let them stand for 10 minutes or more; this will make the skin come off more easily. With a sharp paring knife, peel and core the bell peppers, cut them into long thin strips, and arrange them on a serving dish.

In a small bowl, whisk together the olive oil, lemon juice, cumin, cilantro, parsley, and salt and pepper to taste. Drizzle the dressing over the pepper strips. Serve warm or at room temperature.

SENEGALESE CHICKEN YASSA

Serves 6

This has become my good luck dish. It was one of the first West African dishes that I tasted and it was truly love at first bite. I so love this traditional dish from the Casamance region of southern Senegal that I've demonstrated making it on television and taught it to many folks in cooking classes around the country.

This variation on the classic yassa theme jazzes the dish up a bit by using carrots and pimiento-stuffed olives to create a rich chicken stew.

I often double this recipe because yassa is even better the next day. It also freezes well.

¼ cup fresh lemon juice

¼ cup plus 1 tablespoon peanut oil

4 large onions, thinly sliced

⅛ teaspoon minced fresh habanero or other hot chile, or to taste

Salt and freshly ground black pepper

1 whole chicken (2½ to 3½ pounds), cut into serving pieces

1 whole habanero or other hot chile, pricked with a fork

½ cup pimiento-stuffed olives

4 carrots, peeled and thinly sliced

1 tablespoon Dijon mustard

½ cup water

Plain White Rice (page 60), for serving

In a large nonreactive bowl, combine the lemon juice, ¼ cup of the peanut oil, the onions, minced chile, and salt and pepper to taste. Place the chicken pieces in the marinade, making sure that they are all well covered, and marinate in the refrigerator for at least 2 hours.

Preheat the broiler.

Reserving the marinade and onions, arrange the chicken pieces in a shallow roasting pan. Broil them until they are lightly browned on both sides, about 10 minutes.

Meanwhile, remove the onions from the marinade. In a 3-quart Dutch oven, heat the remaining tablespoon oil over medium heat. Add the onions and cook until tender and translucent, about 5 minutes. Add the remaining marinade and heat through.

When the liquid is thoroughly heated, add the broiled chicken pieces, the whole chile, the olives, carrots, mustard, and water. Stir to mix well, then bring the yassa slowly to a boil over medium heat. Reduce the heat and simmer until the chicken is cooked through, about 20 minutes.

Serve hot over white rice.

PLAIN WHITE RICE

Serves 6 to 8

The real staff of life to many Black Americans, even more than wheat- or corn-based products, is rice; it is a part of our heritage. Many of our ancestors who lived in the area of West Africa known as the Grain Coast were involved in the cultivation of a native African rice (*Oryza glabberima*) long before Europeans arrived on the continent. Their agricultural knowledge was forcibly transported to the Carolinas, where it became the backbone of the Carolina rice industry. Rice is also grown in other parts of the hemisphere; it is astonishing to drive along roads in countries like Haiti and suddenly find rice paddies.

Rice turns up in our meals in all forms, from appetizer fritters to dessert puddings, and is eaten at any time of the day, from breakfast to midnight snack. There are many ways to prepare white rice; this is the simplest.

3⅓ cups water	1 teaspoon salt
1⅓ cups uncooked rice	1 tablespoon butter

In a medium saucepan, bring the water to a boil over medium heat.

Stir in the rice, salt, and butter. Cover, reduce the heat to low, and simmer until the rice is tender, about 20 minutes. Remove the pan from the heat and allow it to stand, covered, for 5 minutes, until all of the water has been absorbed.

Fluff the rice into a serving bowl with a fork and serve hot with additional butter or gravy.

PIMENT AIMÉE (AIMÉE'S HOT SAUCE)

Makes about ½ cup

My friend Aimée is one of the best West African cooks I know. Born in Niger to a Dahomean father and a Nigerien mother, she has traveled the world, living in Paris and various countries of West Africa before finding her current roost in Ouidah, Benin. Aimée's food reflects the influences of all the places she has lived, while maintaining a firm grounding in West African culinary practices. Whatever she serves, whether it's an oh-so-French steak frites or a poulet yassa, she always has a small dish of her homemade chile condiment on the table.

When Aimée comes to visit me in the States, we head first to my greengrocer. There we stock up on habanero chiles so that she can make a small jar of her special piment, which she then packs and takes with her to her other destinations.

10 fresh habanero or other hot chiles

3 cloves garlic, peeled but whole

1 small onion, roughly chopped

½ teaspoon salt, or to taste

In a food processor or blender, combine the chiles, garlic, onion, and salt and pulse until they are a grainy paste. Spoon the paste into a sterilized small jar and cover tightly. The paste will keep for several weeks in the refrigerator and should be used very sparingly as an on-table condiment, or to add extra zing to virtually any dish.

CARAMELIZED RIPE PLANTAINS

Serves 6 to 8

Plantains turn up everywhere in West African cooking. They're nibbled as street snacks, pounded into mashes and foofoos, added to soups and stews, and served as dessert.

Plantains are used at virtually every stage of their maturing process. The green ones are peeled, sliced, and deep-fried as chips. The ripe yellow ones are used as a starch to accompany main dishes, and the superripe black ones in which the starch has turned to sugar appear as desserts. This is one way to serve plantain that appeals to everyone.

4 ripe plantains	1 tablespoon sugar
1 tablespoon butter	

Peel the plantains and slice them into ½-inch rounds.

In a heavy skillet, heat the butter to foaming over medium heat. Add the plantain slices to the butter and cook until they are lightly browned and slightly caramelized, 5 to 8 minutes.

Sprinkle the plantain slices with the sugar, allow the sugar to caramelize slightly, then remove the plantains from the skillet. Serve warm.

Note: These plantain slices are also particularly good when served over vanilla ice cream, topped with the caramelized butter from the pan.

THE NAA NAA MAROCAIN (MOROCCAN MINT TEA)

Serves 6 to 8

Mint tea is served in Morocco and parts of Islamized West Africa. Prepared with much ceremony, it traditionally uses loaf sugar and fresh mint for a taste that is unforgettable and somewhat habit-forming.

This mint tea is a simple one, using lump sugar; it has a teaspoon of dried verbena added to the fresh mint for a different taste. Traditionally, mint tea is served in small glasses that are held with the tips of one's fingers.

4 teaspoons Chinese green tea
1 bunch (6 to 8 sprigs) fresh
  peppermint

1 tablespoon dried verbena
  (see Note)
Sugar lumps

Bring a kettle of water to a boil. Place the tea in a teapot and pour the boiling water over it. Allow the tea to steep for a minute, then add the peppermint, verbena, and sugar lumps to taste. Allow the tea to steep for another minute or so. Serve the tea in small glasses.

In Morocco, the tea is poured from a pot that is held in the air so that the tea is aerated; the sound of the pouring tea adds to the pleasure of drinking.

Note: Available in health food stores.

PROJECT: FAMILY MKEKA

THE MKEKA, OR PLACEMAT, is one of the seven symbols of Kwanzaa. Placed on the Kwanzaa table, the *mkeka* represents tradition, which is the foundation of all knowledge. In keeping with the idea of Kujichagulia, self-determination, the project for the second night of Kwanzaa is to create a family *mkeka*.

Family members should select which of the Nguzo Saba they want to be responsible for and how they will add them to the *mkeka*. They may choose to paint them on, to appliqué them, or to needlepoint or embroider them on. A family decision should be made as to the size of the *mkeka* and of each design, and the fabric that will be used for the background. For large families, each of the Nguzo Saba may become a group project. No member is too young or too old to participate. Feel free to incorporate baby footprints, pieces from special garments, and treasured mementos.

Members may work individually, but on one night they should all assemble to put together the *mkeka*. A family member who is good at needlework should be charged with the finishing touches to the *mkeka*. It will rest proudly on the Kwanzaa table next year and become an heirloom for future generations.

FAMILY PAGE

_____

_____

_____

_____

_____

_____

_____

_____

_____

_____

_____

_____

_____

_____

_____

_____

_____

THE THIRD NIGHT

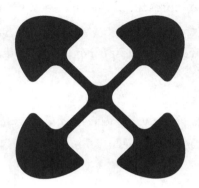

UJIMA
(COLLECTIVE WORK AND RESPONSIBILITY)

to build and maintain our community together
and to make our sisters' and brothers' problems
our problems and to solve them together

He who does not cultivate his field will die of hunger.
—Guinean proverb

On the third night of the holiday, as on all nights of Kwanzaa, the celebration begins with the pouring of the libation from the *kikombe cha umoja* and the lighting of one of the seven candles of the *kinara*. Tonight, the central black candle of Umoja, the first red candle of Kujichagulia, and the first green candle of Ujima (collective work and responsibility) are lighted. After the candles are lighted, the libation is poured or the *kikombe cha umoja* is passed around and thoughts turn to the spirits of those who represented the virtues of Ujima in our society.

Tonight is the night we celebrate the spirit of Ujima (collective work and responsibility).

Tonight, and all nights of the year, we celebrate the spirits of those who have gone before who represent the values of Ujima.

We celebrate the spirits of:
Jomo Kenyatta of Kenya
José Carlos do Patrocino of Brazil
Frantz Fanon of Martinique
Fannie Lou Hamer of the United States
Bayard Rustin of the United States
_____ (your family selection[s])

and the spirits of all others who worked in our communities bringing neighbors and kin together to achieve greater goals.

Tonight, and all nights, we celebrate the spirits of all those who are here with us.

Tonight, and all nights, we celebrate the spirits of those who are yet to come.

JOMO KENYATTA OF KENYA
(1890[?]–1978)

The man who would become Jomo Kenyatta was born to Kikuyu farmers in Negenda in the British East Africa Protectorate in the 1890s. He underwent traditional colonial mission schooling between 1909 and 1914, and in 1914 was baptized under the name of Johnstone Kamau. He would change this name to Kenyatta in the 1920s, after the Mt. Kenya and the name given to the new British colony, as a sign of his increasing political awareness. Active in Kikuyu political organizations, Kenyatta went to London in 1929 as the secretary of the Kikuyu Central Association. In 1931, he returned to London where he studied anthropology at the London School of Economics. In 1938, he published the landmark *Facing Mount Kenya*, a work in which he pioneered the theory of African cultural nationalism. In 1945, he was one of the organizers of the Manchester Pan-African Congress, along with other emerging African leaders like Kwame Nkrumah of Ghana.

Upon his return from England, Kenyatta assumed the mantle of leadership of the Kenya African Union. In Kenya, the Mau Mau guerrilla movement was in full force, and in 1952 a state of emergency was declared by the colonial British authorities. In 1953, following a highly controversial trial, Kenyatta was sentenced to seven years imprisonment. It was a time of trouble during which more than thirteen thousand Africans and one hundred white settlers were killed. During the same turbulent years, over eighty thousand Kikuyu were placed in detention camps. The emergency lasted until 1960. By its end, land reforms had been enacted and Africans directly elected to the legislative council on a restricted franchise. Kenyatta was released from prison in 1961 but was banned from forming a government. In 1963, however, Kenya became a republic with Jomo Kenyatta as its first president. The *mzee*, or old man, as he was affectionately known in his homeland, ruled the country he so loved until his death in 1978.

Tonight, we salute his spirit. We salute the spirit of the *mzee*, Jomo Kenyatta, for bringing a country out of turmoil into nationhood. We salute him for giving peoples of color throughout the world building blocks to cultural nationalism and showing us that we should all truly work together.

JOSÉ CARLOS DO PATROCINIO OF BRAZIL
(1853–1905)

Born in the town of Campos in the state of Rio de Janeiro in 1853, José Carlos do Patrocino was the son of a not-so-celibate priest and a Black vegetable vendor. Through his own heroic efforts, he was able to go to school and to attend university, where he studied and became a writer, pharmacist, orator, and journalist. He was even a pioneer balloonist! A colossus who bestrode his era of Brazilian history, casting a large shadow, he was nicknamed O Gigante Negro da Abolição (The Black Giant of the Abolitionist Movement). Nothing touching on the struggle of Brazilian Blacks for emancipation escaped his hand. Even his detractors conceded that he was a man who was always impassioned and ingenious, and that he expressed himself with a virtuosity of language that was like "a burst of blinding fireworks." A founding member of the Brazilian Academy of Letters, he was also a novelist and a journalist. In keeping with his staunchly abolitionist position, several of his novels dealt with the theme of the evils of slavery. Patrocino was also the founder of the newspaper *A Cidade do Rio de Janeiro* (The City of Rio de Janeiro), which espoused his abolitionist cause.

When, in 1888, Brazil became the last country in the western hemisphere to abolish slavery, Patrocino's antislavery work was done and he declined into semi-oblivion. He died a pauper in 1905 in the Rio de Janeiro that he had so dominated with his personality, but he was not forgotten; over ten thousand people walked in his funeral procession, remembering gratefully the Black Giant of the Abolitionist Movement.

Tonight, we salute his spirit and the insight of a man who truly understood the principle of Ujima. José Carlos do Patrocino, in working to bring freedom to Brazil's children of Africa, knew that in taking responsibility for his brothers and sisters and in helping his community, he was truly helping himself.

FRANTZ FANON OF MARTINIQUE
(1925–1961)

Born July 20, 1925, in Fort-de-France, Martinique, Frantz Fanon attended primary school and the prestigious Lycée Schoelcher. One of his teachers was Aimé Césaire, one of the founders of the Negritude movement. As with most students of his era from the French Caribbean, Fanon, when the time came for higher education, had only one option: schooling in France. But before he undertook that, he fought with the Free French Army during World War II. Then, he attended medical school in Lyon and graduated with a degree in psychiatry. In 1952, the year of his graduation, he published the landmark work *Peau Noire, Masques Blancs* (*Black Skin, White Masks*), a riveting series of observations about the traumas of colonial Black-white relationships.

Fanon's world soon expanded, for in 1953, he was sent to Algeria as director of psychiatric services at Blida-Joinville Hospital. The Algeria to which Fanon journeyed was a land of political upheaval on the verge of a violent overthrow of its colonial masters, the French. It was there that he would find his place as an activist. Fanon published articles in the local press. Expelled from Algeria, he became a member of the press service of the Algerian National Liberation Front in Tunisia.

Profoundly marked by his Algerian experience, Fanon felt at one with the Algerian cause. He saw links between all of the world's oppressed peoples and their fights for freedom. These thoughts would be the catalyst behind his work *Les Damnés de la Terre* (*The Wretched of the Earth*), in which he outlined strategies for all those seeking to fight for freedom, equality, and dignity, strategies that are as valid today as when they were written over sixty years ago. It would be his last completed work. Fanon died of leukemia in the United States under mysterious circumstances in 1961.

Tonight we celebrate the spirit of Frantz Fanon as that of one who understood that the community of oppression is international, transcending nationality race, religion, and gender, and that oppression can only be overcome by the work of all of us together. We celebrate his works that offer us strategies with which to empower our communities, and through our communities, ourselves.

FANNIE LOU HAMER OF THE UNITED STATES
(1917–1977)

No one who lived through the turbulent years of the Civil Rights Movement in the United States will ever forget the face and the voice of Fannie Lou Hamer. Born in 1917 in Montgomery County, Mississippi, she was the youngest of twenty children born to a family of sharecroppers. Hamer knew firsthand the limitations that the world of Jim Crow placed on the Black people of the United States. By the time she was forty-three years old, when she was about to step out onto the stage of history, she was no stranger to adversity and had toiled in the cotton fields of others since the age of six. She had been forced to leave school at age thirteen, and she had also been sterilized: compelled, without her knowledge and without her consent, to give up her right to bear children.

She attended a rally given by the Student Nonviolent Coordinating Committee, where disenfranchised Blacks were asked to volunteer to register to vote. Hamer raised her hand, and after two years of fighting the system, she was finally registered in January 1963. Galvanized, she immediately began helping others to defeat the corrupt system and register to vote. Her activism led her to the vice-chairmanship of the Mississippi Freedom Democratic Party, from there to the Democratic National Convention in Atlantic City, New Jersey, and from there into the minds and consciences of all of America. Her stirring words describing the horrors of racism in her home state of Mississippi and her personal past captured the attention of the nation. A formidable orator who spoke from her heart with fire and feeling, Fannie Lou Hamer crystallized the thoughts of hundreds of thousands of Black Americans when she said simply and eloquently, "I'm just sick and tired of being sick and tired."

We celebrate her spirit tonight as one who honored the principle of Ujima. Uneducated, poor, and Black, she worked from and for her community. She used the tools she had—her homegrown wisdom, her heartfelt eloquence, and her unflagging courage—to change the system for herself and all others.

BAYARD RUSTIN OF THE UNITED STATES
(1912–1987)

Born in West Chester, Pennsylvania, in 1912, Bayard Rustin was a man who lived much of his life in the shadow of others. However, from that penumbra, he worked assiduously to create a better world for all. Rustin was raised as a Quaker and the religion's doctrine of pacifism would affect his entire life. His family was involved with Civil Rights activism, and he would follow suit, studying at Cheyney State Teachers College, Wilberforce University, and the City University of New York. He was a man of diverse interests and even spent some time in New York City singing spirituals in night clubs. In the 1940s, he met Asa Phillip Randolph, the head of the powerful Brotherhood of Sleeping Car Porters, and over the years Rustin became Randolph's strategic genius, working with him on the Journey of Reconciliation designed to test the Supreme Court's ruling on segregation in interstate travel. That journey would result in Rustin's spending twenty-two days on a chain gang and would serve as a model for subsequent Freedom Rides. His strategic genius and behind-the-scenes advisory roles in the Civil Rights Movement would culminate in his work as overall logistical planner for and deputy director of the team that created the 1963 March on Washington for Jobs and Freedom: a centerpiece of the Civil Rights movement.

Rustin, though, while instrumental in creating and implementing that strategies that would make the historic March such a resounding success, always remained behind the scenes, for Bayard Rustin openly and unapologetically lived his life as a gay man, something that was frowned on by some of the movement's leaders and by the prevailing cultural norms of the time. Arrested "for moral cause" early in his career and publicly outed, he chose to remain in background roles, not from shame or fear, but because he never wanted people's opinions about his sexuality to have a negative effect on the Civil Rights movement.

Following the 1964 passage of the Civil Rights Act and the 1965 passage of the Voting Rights Act, Rustin's focus turned more to Human Rights; he served on humanitarian missions to Southeast Asia and Haiti in the 1970s. By the 1980s, Rustin turned his focus to what was then called the Gay Rights movement and worked as an LGBTQ+ advocate and AIDS activist testifying on behalf of New York State's Gay Rights Bill stating, "Gay people are the new barometer for social change."

Tonight, we salute Bayard Rustin for being always unapologetically and unflinchingly himself. We salute him for using his strategic brilliance and his organizational talents—and spending a lifetime doing so—to ensure that everyone regardless of race, gender, or sexual orientation had a voice in the discussion and a seat at the collective table.

The meal celebrating the Nguzo Saba of Ujima is a bring-a-dish potluck supper for family and friends. All of the dishes on tonight's menu can be packed away and taken elsewhere for a larger communal supper.

Appetizer
Grilled Shrimp with Pili Pili Sauce (page 78)

Salad
Romaine Salad with Orange and Radish (page 79)

Main Dish
Herbed Chicken Thighs (page 80)

Vegetables
"Stir-Fried" Broccoli with Garlic (page 81)

Carrots with Ginger (page 82)

Starch
Spicy Three-Cheese Macaroni and Cheese (page 83)

Dessert
Deep-Dish Apple Cobbler (page 85)

Beverage
Pink Party Punch (page 87)

GRILLED SHRIMP WITH PILI PILI SAUCE

Serves 6 to 8 as an appetizer

In coastal areas of Western Africa, Brazil, the Caribbean, and the southern United States, shrimp usually are eaten boiled or grilled with a bit of extra zing given by a hot sauce. This recipe grills the shrimp in the broiler and then serves them with an accompanying hot sauce.

Marinated Shrimp

½ cup fresh lemon juice

1 clove garlic, minced

1 small onion, minced

Salt and freshly ground black pepper

2 pounds jumbo shrimp, peeled and deveined

Pili Pili Sauce

1 small red bell pepper, cut up and seeded

¼ teaspoon minced habanero or other hot chile, or to taste

Marinate the shrimp: In a nonreactive bowl, combine the lemon juice, garlic, onion, and salt and pepper to taste. Reserve 3 tablespoons of the marinade for the pili pili sauce. Add the shrimp, cover with plastic wrap, and marinate in the refrigerator for at least 2 hours.

Preheat the broiler.

When ready, remove the shrimp and arrange them on a wire rack set over a sheet pan. Broil until the shrimp are tender, 2 to 3 minutes.

Make the pili pili sauce: In a blender or food processor, combine the reserved marinade, bell pepper, and chile and pulse until you have a thin paste. Place the sauce in a small bowl, adjust the seasonings to taste.

Serve the shrimp hot with toothpicks and pili pili sauce.

ROMAINE SALAD WITH ORANGE AND RADISH

Serves 6 to 8

In my house, no meal is complete without a salad. To keep friends—and myself—from being bored, I vary the salads with new ingredients and new dressings. This salad was inspired by a traditional Moroccan salad but has the addition of romaine lettuce and a classic vinaigrette with the surprise of a hint of orange juice.

3 large navel oranges

1 bunch globe radishes

2 small heads romaine lettuce, rinsed and torn into bite-size pieces

1½ tablespoons red wine vinegar

5 tablespoons extra virgin olive oil

Salt and freshly ground black pepper

Peel the oranges carefully over a small bowl, reserving the juice. Run a sharp knife along the edge of the membrane separating the orange segments and around each segment. The membrane will come away, leaving an unencumbered orange segment.

Add the orange segments to a large glass salad bowl. Squeeze the remaining orange pulp into the bowl with your hands to retain all of the juice; measure out 1 tablespoon orange juice and set aside.

Reserving 3 or 4 larger radishes for garnish, slice the remaining radishes into rounds and add to the salad bowl. Add the lettuce to the bowl.

In a small bowl, whisk together the reserved orange juice, vinegar, olive oil, and salt and pepper to taste. Grate the reserved radishes over the salad and drizzle the salad dressing over it. Serve at once.

HERBED CHICKEN THIGHS

Serves 6

In all areas of Africa and the diaspora, chicken is eaten fried, boiled, baked, sautéed, and roasted. This dish is easy to prepare and is perfect for a take-along supper because it tastes as good piping hot as it does after it has cooled to room temperature. Instead of being fried, the chicken is marinated in lemon juice and olive oil, covered with a crust of herbs, and broiled. Any type of chicken can be cooked this way, but chicken thighs taste best to me. I allow two chicken thighs per person, but size and hunger will determine how many you need. I also usually cook a double batch because they are great the next day.

2 tablespoons extra virgin olive oil

3 tablespoons fresh lemon juice

2 tablespoons dried thyme

1 tablespoon dried oregano

Salt and freshly ground black pepper

12 medium chicken thighs

In a nonreactive medium bowl, combine the olive oil, lemon juice, 1 tablespoon thyme, 1½ teaspoons oregano, and salt and pepper to taste. Add the chicken thighs, making sure that they are well covered with the marinade. Cover the bowl with plastic wrap and refrigerate for 1 hour.

When ready to cook, preheat the broiler. Set a wire rack in a sheet pan

In a shallow bowl, whisk together the remaining 1 tablespoon thyme and 1½ teaspoons oregano. Remove the chicken thighs from the marinade and roll them in the herbs.

Place the thighs on the rack and broil until they are well browned and fully cooked (no pink chicken, please!), 5 to 7 minutes per side. The herbs will be slightly blackened, but the taste will be ambrosial.

Note: If you aren't planning on cooking all the chicken thighs, you can keep them in the marinade for a day or so in the refrigerator. Or if you want to cook all of them to have leftovers, they can be refrigerated and served at room temperature or sliced into strips and tossed in a mixed or green salad for a great low-cal lunch.

"STIR-FRIED" BROCCOLI WITH GARLIC

Serves 6 to 8

This quick way with broccoli is a change from the usual steamed vegetable. Not stir-fried in the traditional Chinese manner, it is actually pan-fried and then briefly steamed. The crunch of the minced bits of garlic and the subtle taste of sesame oil make the combination a sure winner.

2 heads broccoli

1½ tablespoons sesame oil

4 cloves garlic, cut into thin slivers

1 teaspoon water

Break the broccoli into florets. Peel the stems and cut them crosswise into ½-inch pieces.

In a heavy cast-iron skillet or a wok, heat the sesame oil over medium heat. When the oil is hot, add the garlic slivers and cook them, stirring rapidly, until they are golden brown and crisp. Be careful. The transition time from crisp to charred is seconds. Remove the garlic slivers and drain them on paper towels.

Add the broccoli to the oil and cook for 3 minutes, then drain off the oil, and add the water. Cover and steam until the broccoli is cooked but still crunchy, about 2 minutes.

Serve the broccoli hot sprinkled with the reserved garlic bits.

CARROTS WITH GINGER

Root vegetables are winter standbys on the vegetable table. Though many folks whine when served rutabagas and pout over parsnips, one root vegetable that generally meets with universal approval is carrots. Here, they're simply cooked in a little orange juice with a bit of ginger and freshly grated nutmeg to give them more character.

1 bunch carrots peeled and cut into ½-inch rounds	½ cup fresh orange juice
	Salt and freshly ground black pepper
1 thumb-size piece fresh ginger, scraped and minced	Freshly grated nutmeg
	1 tablespoon butter

In a medium saucepan, combine the carrots, ginger, and orange juice. Cover and cook over medium heat until the carrots are fork-tender, about 10 minutes. Reserving the cooking liquid, drain the carrots and season with salt, pepper, and nutmeg to taste.

In a small saucepan, melt the butter over low heat. Add the reserved cooking liquid and stir until combined.

Drizzle the butter/orange juice mixture over the carrots and serve hot.

SPICY THREE-CHEESE MACARONI AND CHEESE

Serves 6

No winter potluck supper table would be complete without a casserole of macaroni and cheese. Traditionally, the dish is prepared with Cheddar cheese or American cheese. It has also been known to be the delicious final resting place for more than one package of the infamous government cheese that is provided to Welfare recipients. In this recipe, the traditional Cheddar-cheese dish meets up with the Black American love for things hot and well-seasoned, resulting in the addition of pepper Jack, a bit of Parmesan, and a dash of hot sauce.

3 tablespoons unsalted butter

Salt

1½ cups medium elbow macaroni

2 tablespoons all-purpose flour

¾ cup milk

¾ cup freshly grated extra-sharp
  Cheddar cheese

½ cup freshly grated pepper
  Jack cheese

¼ cup freshly grated Parmesan
  cheese

1 teaspoon hot sauce, or to taste

Freshly ground black pepper

¼ cup fine dried bread crumbs

Preheat the oven to 350°F. Lightly grease a 1½-quart baking dish with 1 tablespoon of the butter.

In a pot of boiling salted water, cook the macaroni until tender but still firm according to the package directions. Drain it and place it in the greased baking dish.

In a small saucepan, melt the remaining 2 tablespoons butter over medium heat. Whisk in the flour and cook until the mixture is thick and pasty, about 2 minutes. Gradually drizzle in the milk, whisking constantly, and cook until the sauce has thickened, 7 to 8 minutes. Remove the white sauce from the heat but keep it warm.

Measure out 1 tablespoon of each of the cheeses and set aside in a small bowl. Add the remaining cheese to the white sauce and stir in until smooth. (You may have to return the pan to the stove over low heat to melt the cheeses.) Add the hot sauce and season with black pepper to taste. Pour the sauce over the macaroni in the baking dish and stir it well to make sure that everything is well mixed. Add the bread crumbs to the 3 tablespoons reserved cheese, mix them well, and sprinkle the crumb/cheese mixture over the top of the macaroni.

Bake until hot, bubbling, and lightly browned on the top, 35 to 40 minutes. Serve hot.

DEEP-DISH APPLE COBBLER

Serves 6 to 8

Cobblers appear on African-Atlantic lunch and dinner tables, at church suppers, and outdoor barbecues. They are prepared from whatever fresh fruit is handy; and when there's no fresh fruit, they're even occasionally prepared from dried or preserved fruits. This cobbler is a winter staple that uses apples, which are usually readily available. Traditionally, cobbler is served in small bowls with a bit of crust, the warm apples, and their liquid. Those who want a real treat can top it with a bit of vanilla ice cream and a dusting of brown sugar.

Softened butter for the baking dish

12 medium Granny Smith or other cooking apples, peeled and cut into ¼-inch slices

1 cup packed light brown sugar

1 teaspoon fresh lemon juice

1 tablespoon cold butter

1 teaspoon ground cinnamon

1 teaspoon freshly grated nutmeg

8- or 9-inch unbaked pie crust, store-bought or homemade (recipe follows)

Preheat the oven to 375°F. Generously butter a 9-inch round deep dish.pie pan

Place the apple slices, brown sugar, and lemon juice in the baking dish. Dot the apples with the butter and season them with the cinnamon and nutmeg.

Roll the pie dough out on a floured surface. Cut out a round the size of the top of the baking dish, with enough overlap to seal to the edges of the dish. Trim the scraps and place them in with the apples. Place the crust on top of the apples, covering the top of the baking dish. Seal it to the top of the dish and flute the edges by pinching them between your thumb and forefinger. Slash two or three steam vents in the crust with a sharp knife.

Bake until the crust is golden brown, about 30 minutes.

Serve hot.

BASIC PIE DOUGH

Makes 1 (8- or 9-inch) single crust pie shell

This is the holiday, so only the true pie purist will tell if you cheat a bit and use a prepared pie crust or a pie crust mix. (If so, select the best!) However, for the pie crust purists among us, here's a recipe for a flaky basic pie crust.

1 cup all-purpose flour
½ teaspoon salt

⅓ cup chilled lard or vegetable shortening
2 or 3 tablespoons cold water

In a medium bowl, mix the flour and salt. Cut the lard or shortening into the mixture with a pastry blender or two knives until it has the consistency of cornmeal. Slowly add 2 tablespoons of the water to the mixture, using a fork to mix it in until it becomes a dough. If the dough seems too crumbly, add the remaining water a bit at a time (but remember the trick to a flaky pie crust is to handle it as little as possible). Flatten the dough into a disk, wrap it in wax paper, and refrigerate for at least 30 minutes.

When ready to use, remove the dough from the refrigerator and roll it out on a floured surface as directed in the recipe.

PINK PARTY PUNCH

Serves 8 to 10

All manner of beverages turn up at parties and potluck suppers, from doctored-up pitchers of Kool-Aid to fancy minted lemonades. This pink party punch is a crowd-pleaser that is perfect for the underage set, those who are designated drivers, and those who just plain don't drink alcohol.

1 (16 ounce) package frozen
    strawberries
2 cups fresh orange juice

2 tablespoons fresh lime juice
2 tablespoons grenadine
4 cups ginger ale
Ice

In a blender or food processor, blend the frozen strawberries until they are liquid.

In a large pitcher, combine the strawberry puree, orange juice, lime juice, and grenadine. Add the ginger ale and ice, stir well, and serve.

PROJECT: TEACHING SHARING

THE PROVERB SELECTED FOR this third night of Kwanzaa says, "He who does not cultivate his field will die of hunger." These fields are not only literal but also metaphorical. Tonight is the time to consider cultivating the fields of our communities around the country and around the world. Hunger, the second part of the proverb, is an all too real bogeyman in many of our communities, affecting millions of men, women, and children.

Tonight's project is to work to alleviate that hunger. In creating your own potluck supper tonight to share with family and friends, ask each invited guest to bring along a second dish to be shared with the homeless shelter, AIDS hospice, senior citizens' center, or other group of your choice, or deliver the dishes' ingredients to a food pantry. When you bring the dishes or groceries, take the children of the family along and explain to them why you are doing this. Make this journey not simply a once-a-year Kwanzaa excursion, but a part of your weekly or monthly routines. In that way, we can pass along not only the tales told around the *kinara* each night of Kwanzaa, but also establish and perpetuate the tradition of collective work and responsibility that underlie the Nguzo Saba of this third night: Ujima.

FAMILY PAGE

_____

_____

_____

_____

_____

_____

_____

_____

_____

_____

_____

_____

_____

_____

_____

_____

THE FOURTH NIGHT

UJAMAA

(COOPERATIVE ECONOMICS)

to build and maintain our own stores,
shops, and other businesses and
to profit from them together

It is no shame to work for money.
—Ashanti proverb

On the fourth night of Kwanzaa, as on all other nights of the holiday, the celebration begins with the question *Habari gani?* The answer is *Ujamaa* (cooperative economics). The asking of the Kwanzaa question is followed by the lighting of the candles of the *kinara* and the pouring of the libation from the *kikombe cha umoja.* Tonight, first the central black candle of Umoja, then the first red candle of Kujichagulia, then the first green candle of Ujima are lighted. The second red candle, the candle of Ujamaa is lighted for the first time. After the candles are lighted, the libation is poured or the *kikombe cha umoja* is passed around and thoughts turn to the spirits of those who represented the virtues of Ujamaa in our communities.

Tonight is the night we celebrate the spirit of Ujamaa (cooperative economics).

Tonight, and all nights of the year, we celebrate the spirits of those who have gone before who represent the values of Ujamaa.

We celebrate the spirits of:
Julius Nyerere of Tanzania
Natalino José do Nascimento of Brazil
Violetta Symphort of Guadeloupe
John Merrick of the United States
Brian Williamson of Jamaica
_____ (your family selection[s])

and the spirits of all others who worked in our communities to visualize, establish, create, and nurture economic organizations that enabled all of us to prosper.

Tonight, and all nights, we celebrate the spirits of all those who are here with us.

Tonight, and all nights, we celebrate the spirits of those who are yet to come.

JULIUS NYERERE OF TANZANIA
(1922–1999)

Julius Nyerere's powerful doctrine of cooperative economics is one that we all need to survive. Born the son of a chief in what was then northwestern Tanganyika, Julius Nyerere was educated at government schools in that country. He received his degree in education from Makerere College in Uganda and taught for several years in Tanganyika. He journeyed to Edinburgh, Scotland, to study, received his MA degree from Edinburgh University in 1952, and returned to Tanganyika to teach. In 1954, he was a founding member of the Tanganyika African National Union (TANU). By 1955, he had abandoned teaching to devote his efforts full-time to campaigning for independence and to political organizing. He moved up the political ranks, and when Tanganyika became independent in December 1961, he became the country's first prime minister. He resigned this post six weeks later over political differences to devote himself completely to TANU. In October of the following year, however, when Tanganyika became a republic, he returned as the country's first president. He subsequently became the first president of Tanzania, the union of Tanganyika and Zanzibar, in 1965.

Nyerere was an innovative statesman whose policies stressed rural development for his country and the need for all to work together. Living simply, without pomp and ceremony, Nyerere focused on his belief that in order for us to develop and prosper, we must depend on ourselves, on our own resources, and on our own abilities. Today, Nyerere is a controversial political figure winning respect for his anticolonial stand and the stability that he created in Tanzania, as well as criticism for advocating for a one-party state and other practices. However, today in Tanzania, he is honored with the Swahili honorific *Mwalimu* (teacher).

Tonight, we salute the spirit of Nyerere for teaching us that our past and our future are in each of us and that in order to better ourselves, we must better each other. We salute him for making us all truly learn the meaning of the word *harambee* (let us pull together!), for without it we have no future.

NATALINO JOSÉ DO NASCIMENTO OF BRAZIL
(1905–1975)

Most who experience the thunder of the drums, the volume of the music, and the tidal-wave crowds of hip-shaking samba dancers that make up Carnival in Rio de Janeiro, Brazil, would not think that the festival that has become one of the world's best known has its origins in neighborhood organizations. Yet that is really what Rio's famous samba schools are. One of the early heroes of Rio's samba schools was Natalino José do Nascimento, known simply as Natal.

Natal experienced the extremes of poverty that is the norm for those living in the *favelas*, or shanty towns, that dot the hillsides over Rio de Janeiro. Where there is poverty, there are dreams. Where there are dreams and no money, there are lotteries. Following an accident that resulted in his arm being amputated, and with no trade of his own to ply, Natal became a numbers man for the Brazilian clandestine numbers game: the *Jogo de Bicho* (Animal Game) in 1928. Natal was tough and soon became the virtual uncrowned king of his neighborhood. Unlike most of his fellow *bicheros*, or numbers bankers, Natal did not squander his money. Instead, he financed his samba school, Portela, and donated large amounts of money for the construction of recreational and athletic facilities in his neighborhood. He himself declared his Robin Hood–like theory of life: "Some of my money went to my family, some to the [samba] school, and the rest I would give to people who needed it."

Tonight we salute the spirit of Natal because, despite his human faults, he understood the virtue of Ujamaa. He worked to build his community and to offer more opportunities to those who lived in it. Rooted in the reality of his life, he nonetheless understood the proverb that states: "Through others I am somebody."

VIOLETTA SYMPHORT OF GUADELOUPE
(19??–1991)

Africa lives on in the western hemisphere in many guises. There are secret societies and fraternal lodges, social and pleasure clubs, and coming-of-age rituals. We have our *sousous* and our box hands as alternative savings institutions, and our burial societies as alternative insurance companies.

The Société Saint-Laurent of Guadeloupe is a society formed by the cooks of Guadeloupe as a self-help organization, collecting small amounts of money from members to assure them that when they are ill or unable to work, they will be taken care of. The Société also assures members that they will have a proper funeral. A past president of this Société was a woman known as Violetta Symphort.

Born on the island of Guadeloupe to a culinary family, Violetta Symphort was destined to cook. Learning from her mother and relatives, over the years she developed a mastery of the secrets of the classic Creole cuisine that is so much a part of Guadeloupe. She learned to prepare the *court bouillons* and the *blaffs*, to make the *matété* and the *mignan*. Slowly, she worked her way through the kitchens of the island and from the kitchens into her own restaurant. Her restaurant grew and prospered, and she grew in importance to the community, becoming a virtual culinary ambassadress for her country.

Her personal financial success was assured, yet she retained membership in the Société Saint-Laurent. When she died, she was given a funeral in keeping with her Roman Catholic faith and the ceremonies of the Société Saint-Laurent.

We salute the spirit of Violetta Symphort tonight as one person who never forgot her origins. We recognize her and the Société that she headed as a link with our past, and the cooperative economics that it practiced as a signpost for our future.

JOHN MERRICK OF THE UNITED STATES
(1859–1919)

Born enslaved near Clinton, North Carolina, in 1859, John Merrick grew up at a time when most Black folk were concerned with getting from day to day and had no thoughts of saving for the future or providing for their burial and those they would leave behind. During the period of enslavement, these things were taken care of by the masters and, following Emancipation, in most cases times were too hard for most folks to worry. Tradition had it that widows and orphans were helped by their families aided by their communities. Collections were taken up and saucer burials—where each attendee dropped a few hard-earned coins into a saucer to aid in the proper burial of the deceased—were the norm.

John Merrick knew hard times well. At age twelve, he was sent to work as a laborer in a brickyard in Chapel Hill and there began to learn a trade that would stand him in good stead. He also learned how to read, write, and calculate. After six years at the brickyard, his family moved to Raleigh where he again found work as a brick mason, but jobs became scarce, and he had to find other work. He did, as a bootblack in a barber shop. While he shined shoes, he learned the trade of barbering and soon became a partner and eventually the owner of a barbershop in the county seat of the newly created county of Durham, North Carolina. Merrick's fortunes continued to improve; the one shop became five barbershops, and he began to invest in real estate in the town, which grew rapidly as people poured into it to work in the tobacco factories.

Merrick's personal wealth grew along with the town, but he never lost touch with his customers or with his desire to work for community betterment. No one knows exactly why Merrick and six of his friends decided to begin an industrial insurance business, but in 1898 the North Carolina Mutual and Provident Association was incorporated by the State of North Carolina. The company's motto, "Merciful to All," spoke more to the desires of Merrick and the other founders than anything else. A portion of the company's proceeds was to be turned over to the Colored Orphan Asylum in Oxford, North Carolina. The company that Merrick began was a pioneer in providing mortgages for Black Americans around the country, in aiding the creation of new businesses, and in generally helping Black Americans keep their dreams alive. Merrick died in 1919 and the company lived on until 2022 when it entered liquidation.

Tonight, we salute John Merrick for his business acumen, for his ability to triumph over adversity, to rise and thrive and prosper. We salute him for knowing that no Black American business is truly successful unless it helps us all learn and succeed. We salute him as one who truly knew the meaning of Ujamaa and who used it to help us all grow.

BRIAN WILLIAMSON OF JAMAICA
(1945-2004)

Anyone who journeys to Jamaica knows that it is an island of lush beauty: high mountains, cascading waterfalls, and spectacular beaches that lure visitors from all over the world. Most people who journey to Jamaica do not know that the beautiful island and many others in the Caribbean region can also be profoundly homophobic. Jamaica has a reputation for antigay prejudice that is witnessed at all levels of discourse, both public and private. A Gay March announced as a joke on the radio brought along the rumored parade route bands of citizens with cutlasses (as machetes are called there) and other weapons determined to kill or harm what they call in Jamaica a batty man (*batty* means backside in Jamaican patois).

Brian Williamson was born there into a comfortable family in Saint Anne's parish, the largest of Jamaica's fourteen parishes and the location of the tourist enclave of Ocho Rios. Williamson originally thought of becoming a Roman Catholic priest and began studying for the priesthood in Montego Bay, but decided against it. In 1979, he turned to LGBTQ+ activism, becoming one of the first openly gay men in Jamaica. He initially offered his apartment as a safe space where other gay men could gather every other week. By the early 1990s he had bought a compound in the New Kingston section of the country's capital city and transformed part of it into the country's first gay nightclub, called Entourage, even though same-sex relationships were, and still are, illegal in Jamaica. It remained open for two years.

In 1988, Williamson, along with other members of the LGBTQ+ community, formed an organization: the Jamaican Forum for Lesbians, All Sexuals, and Gays (J-FLAG) that advocated for legal reform, created educational and social programs, and recorded anti-LGBTQ+ crimes including more than thirty reputed murders of gay men between 1997 and 2004. While others remained anonymous, Williamson, the face of a nascent movement, repeatedly came under threat to the degree that he moved to Canada and England for his safety. After returning to live in his compound in Jamaica in 2004, despite the risk, he was brutally killed in his apartment in New Kingston. It has been called "the most prominent example of an antigay murder on the island." His murderer was sentenced to prison for life.

We salute Brian Williamson this evening for his courage that allowed him to openly live his life while helping others live theirs. We salute him because he set his face against the prevailing social culture of his country and worked to create a safe community for his people.

The menu celebrating the Nguzo Saba of Ujamaa is a formal meal
for business networking. It can be used during Kwanzaa as a meal for friends
to come together to discuss business plans and ideas, or at any time of the
year to entertain business contacts and clients.

Appetizer
Broiled Grapefruit with Rum (page 101)

Salad
Endive with Pears and Roquefort (page 102)

Main Dish
Pecan-Coated Roast Loin of Pork with Baked Peaches (page 103)

Condiment
Peach Apricot Chutney (page 105)

Vegetables
Garlic-Sesame String Beans (page 106)
Baked Potatoes with Spiced Yogurt (page 107)

Dessert
Sautéed Bananas with Rum Raisin Sauce (page 108)

Beverage
Caribbean Sorrel (page 109)

BROILED GRAPEFRUIT WITH RUM

Serves 6

This appetizer is simple, but it makes a perfectly delicious opening statement. With the addition of rum and a bit of brown sugar, the ordinary grapefruit half is transformed into something that signals a festive meal to come.

3 ruby red grapefruit

¼ cup packed dark brown sugar

¼ cup rum, or to taste

Preheat the broiler.

Cut the grapefruit in half through the equator and use a sharp knife to separate the individual segments from the membranes by running the knife around each small triangular section. Lift the sections out slightly, and then return them.

Sprinkle a bit of brown sugar on each grapefruit half and drizzle on the rum. Place the grapefruit in a baking dish that will fit into your broiler and broil them until the sugar has melted and the grapefruit halves are slightly browned on the top, about 5 minutes.

Serve hot.

ENDIVE WITH PEARS AND ROQUEFORT

Serves 6

The combination of Belgian endive, ripe Anjou pears, and Roquefort, the king of the blue cheeses, is just ambrosial. This recipe mixes them together with a dash of a classic vinaigrette for a winter salad that's absolutely elegant.

3 small heads Belgian endive, separated into leaves

2 medium firm-ripe Anjou pears, cored and thinly sliced lengthwise

⅓ cup crumbled Roquefort cheese (see Note)

¼ teaspoon Dijon mustard

⅔ cup olive oil

3 tablespoons red wine vinegar

1 tablespoon balsamic vinegar

Pinch of sugar

Salt and freshly ground black pepper

Arrange the endive and the pear slices on six individual salad plates and sprinkle them with the crumbled Roquefort cheese.

In a small bowl, whisk together the mustard, olive oil, both vinegars, the sugar, and salt and pepper to taste. Drizzle it over the salads. Serve at once.

Notes:
- If you cannot find Roquefort, you may substitute any good blue cheese.
- The salad dressing may be prepared in advance and kept in the refrigerator until needed. If so, whisk well before using.

PECAN-COATED ROAST LOIN OF PORK WITH BAKED PEACHES

Serves 8

The traditional roast pork is given a Southern accent with a crust of well-seasoned crushed pecans. Thinly sliced pork loin with a slathering of the Peach Apricot Chutney (page 105) makes perfect sandwiches the following day to take to work or school.

The savory baked peaches are the perfect accompaniment to winter roasts. If there are only a few guests at the table, you may wish to serve a bit of the peach apricot chutney in the hollow of each of the baked peaches. If the guests are more numerous, serve the peaches as a side dish with the meat.

Roast Pork

4 pounds boneless pork loin

¼ cup olive oil, plus more as needed

1 tablespoon dark brown sugar

2 teaspoons rubbed sage

1 teaspoon dried thyme

1 teaspoon minced garlic

Salt and freshly ground black pepper

4 ounces pecans

Baked Peaches

8 canned freestone peach halves
  (the number varies from can to can,
  regardless of weight, so check!)

2 tablespoons dark brown sugar

Freshly grated nutmeg

Rub the pork loin with the olive oil, making sure that it is well covered.

In a food processor or blender, combine the brown sugar, sage, thyme, garlic, and salt and pepper to taste and pulse until you have a thick paste. You may have to add a drizzle of olive oil to get it started. Slather the paste all over the pork loin, cover it with plastic wrap, and refrigerate it overnight.

Preheat the oven to 400°F.

In a food processor or blender, pulse the pecans until they are finely chopped. Roll the pork loin in the crushed pecans and place it in a roasting pan. Make a tent of aluminum foil and arrange it over the pork loin, covering the nuts completely so that they won't char.

Roast for 30 minutes. Reduce the oven temperature to 350°F and continue to roast for 60 minutes.

Pull out the pan, and place the peach halves around the roast in the bottom of the roasting pan. Sprinkle the peaches with the brown sugar and a grinding of nutmeg. Remove the foil and continue to roast about 20 minutes longer or until the pork is done (145 to 160°F). Allow to sit for 10 minutes then serve the roast hot with the peaches.

PEACH APRICOT CHUTNEY

Makes about 2 cups

I think that roasted meats always cry for a condiment; my preference is for a home-made chutney. This chutney uses canned peaches and dried apricots; the peaches complement the baked peaches that accompany the pork loin (see page 103), and the habanero chile adds zing.

8 ounces dried apricots

6 canned freestone peach halves, drained

⅛ teaspoon minced habanero or other hot chile, or to taste

1-inch piece fresh ginger, scraped

Pinch of ground cloves (grind them yourself for the best flavor)

1 cup sugar

1 cup cider vinegar

In a medium bowl, soak the apricots in water to cover for 1 hour. Reserving ¼ cup of the soaking liquid, drain the apricots. In a food processor, combine the apricots, the reserved soaking liquid, the peach halves, chile, ginger, and cloves and pulse until you have a thick paste.

Place the paste in a nonreactive saucepan and stir in the sugar and vinegar. Bring to a boil over medium heat, then reduce the heat and cook until the mixture reaches a jamlike texture, stirring occasionally to make sure that the chutney does not stick to the bottom of the saucepan or scorch. It will take about 40 minutes, but cooking time will vary. Just keep cooking until you have the correct consistency.

Spoon the chutney into sterilized glass jars and refrigerate if you are using it within a week. If you're preparing a large batch to share with friends or to store, process according to proper canning methods.

GARLIC-SESAME STRING BEANS

Serves 6 to 8

Most folk would think that this vegetable dish has an Asian overtone. Perhaps it does, but others think sesame seeds are African in origin, so I guess we could stake a claim as well. In any case, this recipe gives a new twist to plain old string beans.

2 pounds unblemished green beans, trimmed

2 tablespoons unsalted butter

1 tablespoon minced garlic, or to taste

2 tablespoons toasted sesame seeds

Bring a 2-quart saucepan of water to a rolling boil. Plunge the beans into the water and cook until they are firm-tender and crisp, 5 to 7 minutes. Drain the beans and set aside.

In a medium skillet, heat the butter over low heat until foamy. Add the garlic and the sesame seeds and cook, stirring constantly, until the garlic is lightly browned, about 3 to 5 minutes.

Add the beans and continue to cook, stirring constantly, until the beans are completely coated with the garlic and sesame seeds. Serve hot.

BAKED POTATOES WITH SPICED YOGURT

Serves 8

Just about everyone loves baked potatoes. Most of us add butter and/or sour cream, but this recipe offers a healthier twist. The spiced yogurt is delicious enough that you might just want to eat it with sliced vegetable sticks as a snack by itself. These potatoes can be popped into the oven along with the Pecan-Coated Roast Loin of Pork (page 103), making them not only healthful, but also energy efficient (see Notes). The spicy yogurt can be prepared several hours or even a few days ahead.

1 cup plain yogurt

1 tablespoon minced fresh cilantro (see Note)

3 scallions, chopped, including 2 inches of the green part

½ teaspoon ground cumin

8 medium baking potatoes

In a small bowl, mix the yogurt, cilantro, scallions, and cumin. Cover with plastic wrap, and place it in the refrigerator for at least 1 hour.

Preheat the oven to 350°F.

Scrub the potatoes and prick them with a fork. Arrange the potatoes directly on the oven racks and bake until fork-tender, about 1 hour to 1 hour 15 minutes.

When the potatoes are ready, split them open and serve each one with a heaping dollop of the spiced yogurt. You won't even miss the butter and sour cream.

Notes:
- Those who despise cilantro can replace it with spearmint for a different taste.
- To bake these along with the loin of pork, stick them in the oven after the pork has been in for 30 minutes.

SAUTÉED BANANAS WITH RUM RAISIN SAUCE

Serves 8

The sweet, slightly creamy taste of bananas just seems to go perfectly with the molasses taste of Caribbean dark rum. In this dessert, similar to New Orleans' Bananas Foster, the ingredients blend to form a dessert that can be a showy finish to any meal.

½ cup dark raisins

¾ cup Caribbean dark rum

8 firm-ripe bananas, halved lengthwise

4 tablespoons (½ stick) unsalted butter

¼ cup packed dark brown sugar

Freshly grated nutmeg

In a small bowl, combine the raisins and the rum and let stand for 30 minutes.

In a large heavy skillet, heat the butter over low heat until foamy. Add the bananas, round-side down and cook for 2 to 3 minutes on each side, turning them carefully so that they do not break. Remove them from the pan, arrange them on a serving platter, and keep them warm.

In the same skillet, add the rum and raisins to the butter remaining in the pan, along with the brown sugar, and nutmeg and heat until warmed through. (At this point you may wish to flambé the rum by carefully lighting it with a long match or a long fire lighter.)

Pour the rum raisin sauce over the bananas and serve at once.

Note: For a super-special dessert, serve the bananas with vanilla or banana ice cream.

CARIBBEAN SORREL

Makes 1 quart

It wouldn't be Christmas in the Caribbean without the roseate beverage known as sorrel. Prepared from the pods of a red flowering plant of the hibiscus family, sorrel is also drunk in West Africa. Senegalese folk savor it as well, but without the additional spices, and call it *bissap rouge*; in Egypt, it is known as *karkade*.

When purchasing sorrel, be careful: You don't want the green leaf known by the French as sorrel; you're looking for dried reddish-brown pods. It may be called hibiscus or *flor de Jamaica*. You can find it in health food stores and in Caribbean markets year-round. You may also find it fresh in Caribbean markets at the holiday season. In the Caribbean, adults drink their holiday sorrel mixed with liberal doses of whatever local rum is their preferred brand. You can drink yours plain or mixed with rum as well. Select a good rum from the English-speaking Caribbean, like Mount Gay, Cockspur, Appelton, or Foursquare.

2 heaping cups dried sorrel pods	1 quart boiling water
5 whole cloves	1 cup superfine sugar, or to taste
1 tablespoon grated orange zest	Several grains uncooked white rice
1 (2-inch) stick cinnamon	Good rum (optional), such as
¼ teaspoon freshly grated nutmeg	Mount Gay, Cockspur, Appleton,
1½ tablespoons grated fresh ginger	or Foursquare

In a large heatproof crock or heavy bowl, combine the sorrel pods, cloves, orange zest, cinnamon, nutmeg, and ginger. Pour the boiling water over them and allow the mixture to steep for 24 hours.

When ready to serve, strain the mixture and add the sugar, stirring well. Pour the sorrel into a sterilized 1-quart jar that can be loosely capped and add the rice. (There are lots of theories about what the rice does, but all agree that the best reason to add it is that it's traditional.) Allow the jar to remain in a cool, dark place for 2 days or longer, then serve.

To serve, dilute the sorrel with an equal volume of water. Whether or not you choose to add rum is strictly up to you.

PROJECT: HOMEMADE NOTECARDS

THE DESIRE FOR FAMILIES to communicate with each other at special times is not one created by Hallmark. The basic human need to share news, good wishes, and hopes with family and friends is something that is universal, especially when our families are increasingly separated and scattered. In this era of text messages and emails, nothing is more fun to receive than a handwritten notecard.

The project for the fourth night of Kwanzaa is to maintain contact with friends and family near and far by means of your own family-created notecards. With a bit of Kuumba, creativity, you can transform a blank piece of paper into your own special message. Get out the crayons, colored pencils, glue gun, and sparkles. Dust off those rubber stamps and stickers, and try to remember where you put the ink pad. This is the time to think about printing out those thousands of photographs that you have stored on your phone and making collages from them and from those magazines that have been sitting in the corner for too long. Put those verses you've been keeping in your head and those you've written on scraps of paper that are scattered around the house to good use. Sit around the kitchen table and snip, clip, and create. Who knows, your cards may be so good that they'll be the start of a family enterprise. What better example of Ujamaa can you think of?

FAMILY PAGES

....

....

....

....

....

....

....

....

....

....

....

....

....

....

....

....

....

FAMILY PAGES

_____

_____

_____

_____

_____

_____

_____

_____

_____

_____

_____

_____

_____

_____

_____

_____

THE FIFTH NIGHT

NIA

(PURPOSE)

to make our collective vocation the building and developing of our community in order to restore our people to their traditional greatness

Before shooting, one must aim.
—Ethiopian proverb

On the fifth night of Kwanzaa, as on all other nights of the holiday, the celebration begins with the question *Habari gani?* The answer is *Nia* (purpose). The asking of the Kwanzaa question is followed by the lightning of the candles of the *kinara* and the pouring of the libation from the *kikombe cha umoja.* Tonight, the second green candle, the candle of Nia, is lighted for the first time. After the candles are lighted, the libation is poured or the *kikombe cha umoja* is passed around, and thoughts turn to the spirits of those who represented the virtues of Nia.

Tonight is the night we celebrate the spirit of Nia (purpose).

Tonight, and all nights of the year, we celebrate the spirits of those who have gone before who represent the values of Nia.

We celebrate the spirits of:
   Abla Poku of the Baoule of the Côte d'Ivoire
   Maria Escolástica da Conceição Nazaré of Brazil
   Toussaint L'Ouverture of Haiti
   Thurgood Marshall of the United States
   Audre Lorde of the United States
   _____ *(your family selection[s]),*

and the spirits of all others who worked, nurtured, and sacrificed so that all of us remember the traditional greatness of our ancestors, a legacy that we must nourish and cherish.

Tonight, and all nights, we celebrate the spirits of all those who are here with us.

Tonight, and all nights, we celebrate the spirits of those who are yet to come.

ABLA POKU OF THE BAOULE OF THE CÔTE D'IVOIRE (17??-1760)

Born in the West African region between the Volta and the Bandama Rivers in the early part of the eighteenth century, Abla Poku was royal on both her mother's and her father's side of the family. Although of royal birth, she did not have an easy childhood, and her young years were punctuated with the turmoil that marked the eighteenth century among the Akan peoples: wars of succession, the sack of Kumasi by Ebri Moro, the murders of many of her family, and her own exile. Poku's position as potential Queen Mother (an important role in Akan society) made her a pawn in the quarrels over the throne.

No one knows how she found the land to which she led her partisans. Some say that she found it during her early exile. But she led an exodus of thousands of Ashanti-Asabou nobles, their vassals, and households on a trek that would take them westward. Along the way, the fleeing nobles were aided by villagers and townspeople who joined the caravan, swelling their numbers. It seemed that the entire group was doomed when they reached the banks of the Komoé River in today's Côte d'Ivoire; there, the size of the river made passage impossible.

Legend has it that on the riverbanks, Queen Poku offered her only child to the waters to ensure the safe passage of her people uttering the words *baa-ouli* ("the child is dead"). The moment of a mother's supreme sacrifice for the good of her people lives on in the new name of the people—*Baoule*. Poku and her sacrifice established a new kingdom in which the Akan matrilineal system of government and the Agoua royal house were assured. When she died in 1760 at Niamonou near what would become the capital of the Baoule kingdom, she had left her mark forever on the history of her people.

We salute the spirit of Queen Abla Poku this evening for her leadership and vision. We honor her for her sense of purpose, her clear focus, and her willingness to offer the supreme maternal sacrifice for the survival of her people.

MARIA ESCOLÁSTICA DA CONCEIÇÃO NAZARÉ OF BRAZIL
(1894–1986)

Born on February 10, 1894, only six years after the formal abolition of slavery in Brazil, Maria Escolástica da Conceição Nazaré was a child with a destiny. Descended from Africans who hailed from the Nigerian town of Abeokuta, she was the great-granddaughter of one of the women who brought the African religion of the Yoruba people to Brazil, where it would evolve into what is known today as Candomblé. Initiated at the age of eight months, she would become the spiritual leader of her religious house, Gantois, at twenty-eight. Born at a time when the religion of her ancestors was reviled as "The Religion of the Blacks" and equated with satanism, she would live to be consulted by statesmen and courted by movie stars, praised in songs written by famous composers, and treated as the uncrowned queen of Salvador da Bahia, Brazil.

A votary of *orixa* of love, coquetry, and rivers known in Brazil as Oxum, Maria Escolástica da Conceição Nazaré became affectionately known through Brazil and beyond its borders as Mae Menininha (Little Girl). Her fame came from her goodness and her strict adherence to the traditions of her religion. She was intransigent about the respect that she demanded and commanded for her religion. During the sixty-four years that Mae Menininha presided over Gantois, Candomblé grew from a religion persecuted by the police and assailed in newspaper editorials to become one of the most potent cultural forces for the betterment of Blacks in Brazil.

Mae Menininha was at the forefront of this evolution. Always open to true conversation with all, her willingness to discuss, but not compromise, to lead, yet not terrorize, and to teach, yet not proselytize, made her, in the terms of one newspaper article, "the virtual Pope of Candomblé." Those who had the honor of sitting at her feet (as I did) knew that they had been in the presence of true saintliness and greatness. When she died in 1986, the city of Salvador da Bahia de Todos os Santos mourned her passing. She was given a state funeral that was attended by all from governors to dressmakers, writers to dockworkers, street vendors to singing stars. Shops closed, the radio played mourning dirges, and her funeral occupied the television. She was Bahia's queen and her equal will not be soon seen again.

Tonight we salute the spirit of Mae Menininha of Gantois for her goodness and her greatness. We salute her for her purpose and her leadership, for standing forth and standing firm, and for knowing that the gentle constant force of a river will wear down rock.

TOUSSAINT L'OUVERTURE OF HAITI
(1743–1803)

Toussaint L'Ouverture was born enslaved on the Bréda plantation in the French colony of Saint-Domingue. Some say that he was the grandson of a Rada chief of Dahomey who was captured and enslaved. As a child, he was frail, but determined, and set about building his endurance so that by the time that he was twelve he was a formidable athlete. Even at age sixty, he rode 125 miles daily on horseback with ease and was known as "the Centaur of the Savannahs." He was not handsome, but he had character, personality, and intellect that set him above other men long before he entered the political scene.

Toussaint worked on the plantation as steward of livestock and then as coachman, positions that honed his skills at management and reinforced his abilities to lead. He could also read, no mean accomplishment during the troubled times at the end of the eighteenth century in Saint-Domingue. Toussaint Bréda joined the revolution late and as an "old" man—he was forty-five—he advanced rapidly to the top ranks.

The deeds of the Haitian Revolution are complex and bloody, and affect the history of that land even today; yet they were the crucible for the birthplace of greatness. Toussaint Bréda became known to the world as Toussaint L'Ouverture (the Opening) for his military ability to open the ranks of his enemies. He rose to the forefront of history through his leadership, his military genius, and his intellect. Fighting for the freedom of others like him, he cut a swath through history. In his ruling of Saint-Domingue, he freed his people, pacified the country, began rebuilding agriculture, and governed fairly. It was not to last. Captured by the treachery of Napoléon Bonaparte, Toussaint L'Ouverture was taken to France and held without trial in a prison in the French Alps, where he died in exile on April 27, 1803.

We salute the indomitable spirit of Toussaint L'Ouverture tonight as one whose sense of purpose changed a world. We salute him as one of the founders of the first independent Black nation in this hemisphere and as one who knew the price of liberty. We salute his spirit tonight on this night of purpose for his purpose and vision in saying to the world, "In overthrowing me, you have cut down in Saint-Domingue only the trunk of the tree of liberty. It will spring up again by the roots, for they are numerous and deep."

THURGOOD MARSHALL OF THE UNITED STATES (1908–1993)

Thurgood Marshall was born in Baltimore, Maryland, in 1908, the grandson of an African-born slave. His father was a steward in a white country club and his mother taught in segregated schools. Educated at Lincoln University in Pennsylvania and at Howard University Law School, Marshall entered private law practice following his graduation.

His interest, though, was in the growing Civil Rights movement, and while he was in law practice, he worked for the National Association for the Advancement of Colored People (NAACP). By 1938, he had become the organization's chief counsel. During the years from 1938 to 1961, when he was appointed to the United States Court of Appeals, he worked on numerous civil rights cases, including ones that led to the admission of the first Black American student to the University of Missouri Law School, the desegregation of interstate passenger carriers in Virginia, and the landmark 1954 *Brown* v. [the Topeka] *Board of Education,* one of the first steps on the road to school desegregation.

Marshall was appointed associate justice of the United States Supreme Court by President Lyndon B. Johnson in 1967. He sat on the Supreme Court until his retirement in 1991. Known among his friends for his wicked wit, when asked the reason for his retirement from the Supreme Court, Marshall simply replied, "Why? Because I'm old!" He *was* old, but his opinions in the area of civil rights were trenchant and timely.

We salute the spirit of Thurgood Marshall this evening because he represents singleness of purpose. Once his focus was aimed at seeing that Black Americans, and indeed *all* Americans, were not deprived of their civil rights, he persevered. His sound judgment and wisdom were tempered with humor and never failed him. He pursued his goals with a sureness of focus and a tenacity of conviction that never flagged. We salute the spirit of Thurgood Marshall this evening, for he truly epitomized Nia.

AUDRE LORDE OF THE UNITED STATES
(1934–1992)

Audre Lorde began life as Audrey Geraldine Lorde in 1934 in New York City. Her family was cursed by the oh-so-Black American vice of colorism, and she had a troubled relationship with her family, especially with her mother who was wary of folks who were darker complected than she was. The youngest of three sisters, Lorde grew up listening to her mother's tales of the Caribbean. She was nearsighted to the point of being almost legally blind and struggled with communication, yet she penned her first poem while in the eighth grade. She loved poetry and it became her major method of communication. She also changed the spelling of her name to Audre Lorde because, as she told it in her work *Zami, a New Spelling of My Name*, she liked the artistic symmetry of the two e's.

Lorde attended New York City's prestigious Hunter College High School and participated in poetry workshops. She studied for a year at the National University of Mexico and returned to NYC where she graduated from Hunter College and received a master's in library science from Columbia all while continuing to write and hone her self-definition as "crazy and queer." Her academic career continued in parallel to her career as a writer and a poet, and she taught in various departments at universities throughout New York City's CUNY system while penning collections of poetry that made her an important voice in the Black Arts movement. Her parallel careers as poet/activist began to take off when her collection *Coal* gained national recognition. She became a co-founder of Kitchen Table: Women of Color Press. By 1981, she was one of the founders of the Women's Coalition of Saint Croix, in the Caribbean, and an increasing presence on the international front all the while continuing to explore her self-definition. She died in 1992 of breast cancer, a disease that also served as catalyst for much of her later work.

We salute Audre Lorde this evening because Lorde used her literary gifts and her commitment as an activist (when the word had real currency) and found purpose in redefining perceptions of what it meant to be a Black woman, lesbian, poet, mother, and feminist for us all.

We salute Audre Lorde for firmly believing that any form of oppression was the oppression of all and that differences should not be exploited to create wedges between diverging groups.

The menu celebrating Nia is a meal reminding us of our ancestors' American presence. It is a meal of the foods of adversity, as transformed by a people whose greatness could not be destroyed.

Appetizer
Spicy Sautéed Pecans (page 124)

Salad
Wilted Winter Salad with Jerusalem Artichokes (page 125)

Main Dish
Roast Chicken (page 127)

Condiment
Spicy Vinegar (page 130)

Vegetables
Baked Sweet Potatoes (page 128)

Home-Style Collards with Spicy Vinegar (page 129)

Dessert
Holiday Gingerbread with Molasses Whipped Cream (page 131)

Beverage
Eggnog (page 133)

SPICY SAUTÉED PECANS

Serves 4

Pecans were a part of the lives of many of our ancestors in the South. In some areas, they were so plentiful that they simply fell from the trees. They are still readily available, and many families receive a sackful of them at the end of the year. Our enslaved ancestors certainly didn't have time for appetizers; they more than likely nibbled on the sweet meat of pecans whenever they could be found. Sautéing the nuts briefly in a bit of butter just seems to bring out that sweetness. This dish adds sugar and the surprise of chili powder to give the pecans an extra zing.

2 cups pecans

3 tablespoons unsalted butter

1 tablespoon chili powder

2 teaspoons light brown sugar

½ teaspoon salt

Pick over the pecans and remove any shells and shriveled nuts. (Just because the package claims the nuts are shelled, you shouldn't believe it. Pick them over!)

In a large cast-iron skillet, heat the butter to foaming over low heat. Add the pecans and cook them for 3 to 5 minutes, stirring them occasionally with a wooden spoon to make sure that they are well coated with butter.

When they are ready, place the chile powder, brown sugar, and salt in a brown paper bag and taste to check seasonings. Add the toasted pecans and shake to coat, then drain on absorbent paper and serve warm.

WILTED WINTER SALAD WITH JERUSALEM ARTICHOKES

Serves 8

Salads were definitely not a regular part of the diet of our ancestors, but they did pick wild greens and eat them in various ways. Jerusalem artichokes, tubers that grow underground, were there for the finding, and were a special treat.

This salad can be made from any hearty wild greens that might be available; it can also be prepared from a mix of watercress and dandelion greens. The dressing uses bacon, but if your family does not eat pork, you can use beef or turkey bacon.

½ pound Jerusalem artichokes,
  well scrubbed
4 slices pork or turkey bacon,
  cut into 1-inch strips
2 tablespoons cider vinegar
1 teaspoon molasses

1 tablespoon water
Salt and freshly ground black
  pepper
1 bunch watercress
1 bunch dandelion greens
1 small red onion, sliced

In a medium saucepan, bring at least 2 cups water to a boil. Add the Jerusalem artichokes, cover, and cook until firm but fork-tender, about 15 minutes. (Cooking time will depend on the size of the individual artichokes, so check occasionally. They may not all be done at the same time.) Drain and when cool enough to handle, thinly slice.

Meanwhile, line a paper plate with paper towels and set near the stove. In a small cast-iron skillet, cook the bacon over medium heat until crisp. Transfer the bacon to the paper towels. Pour off all but 1 tablespoon of the rendered fat.

Return the skillet to low heat. Rapidly add the cider vinegar, molasses, and water and stir well to mix all of the ingredients. Taste and adjust the seasoning. (The flavor of the dressing will depend on the saltiness of your bacon, the tartness of your vinegar, and the brand of your molasses, so taste it.)

In a glass salad bowl, combine the greens, onion slices, and Jerusalem artichokes. Add the bacon to the greens, then pour the dressing over the salad and serve warm.

ROAST CHICKEN

Serves 4

A wonderful Creole proverb states, "When the preacher comes to dinner the chickens cry." Even during the dark years of our enslavement, there were occasional chicken dinners. Then the birds were usually roasted on spits in front of the hearths that were the sole source of heat and light in many of the cabins. Nothing tastes quite like hearth-roasted chicken, but this oven-roasted bird comes close. The next day any leftover chicken can be served in a salad, in sandwiches, or cold with one of the chutneys from the book (see pages 34, 105, and 155).

1 whole chicken (3⅓ to 4 pounds)
3 tablespoons butter
1 medium onion, left whole

1 tablespoon Bell's or other poultry seasoning
Salt and freshly ground black pepper

Preheat the oven to 450°F.

Remove the chicken giblets from the cavity of the chicken. Pat it dry. Cut 1½ tablespoons of the butter into small pieces. Insert the butter pieces under the breast and leg skin of the chicken to keep it tender.

In a small saucepan, melt the remaining 1½ tablespoons butter. Rub the onion with some of the melted butter and place it in the cavity of the chicken. Rub the remaining melted butter, all over the chicken. In a small bowl, stir together the poultry seasoning and salt and pepper to taste. Prepare the mixture over the chicken as well.

Place the chicken in a baking pan and into the oven. After 15 minutes, reduce the heat to 350°F and roast, checking it occasionally, until the chicken juices run clear when pricked with a fork at the leg joint, about 1 hour 15 minutes.

Serve hot.

BAKED SWEET POTATOES

Serves 8

Traditionally, while the dinner chicken was roasting on the spit, the sweet potatoes were slow-cooking in the ashes of the fire. Simply baking sweet potatoes somehow brings out all of their sweetness. Look for the smaller ones—they're sweeter; and remember, even if they call them yams, they're not. (Yams are something else altogether!)

8 small to medium sweet potatoes 2 tablespoons olive oil

Preheat the oven to 375°F.

Scrub the sweet potatoes well (after all, they're grown in the ground and you don't want to eat dirt). Prick them with a fork, rub them with the olive oil.

Place the sweet potatoes on foil in the oven and bake until fork-tender, about 1 hour.

Note: If you are making the Roast Chicken (page 127), place them in the oven with the chicken. They should be done in the time it takes to roast the chicken.

HOME-STYLE COLLARDS WITH SPICY VINEGAR

Serves 6

I am fanatic about greens and I prefer collard greens to all others. The recipe is for collards, but you can use whatever greens you like: kale, turnip, or mustard. Winter is the best time for all greens; some say they taste their best after they're hit by the first frost. When shopping for greens, select the youngest leaves. They will be the most tender; naturally, avoid any yellow or blemished ones.

4 pounds young, leafy collard greens	6 cups water
1 small ham hock (see Note)	Salt and freshly ground black pepper

Condiments

1 onion, minced	Spicy Vinegar (page 130)

Place the greens in a sinkful of cold water and wash them thoroughly. Cut out any discolored spots and the fibrous stem and midrib on all but the smallest leaves.

In a large heavy soup pot, add the greens, ham hock, and water and bring to a boil. Reduce the heat to low and cook until the greens are tender and the meat of the ham hock falls off the bone, 2 hours or longer, adding more water if necessary. Season with salt and pepper.

Don't discard the liquid in which they cooked. That's the "pot likker" and is served with the greens. Some can be served in a sauce boat so diners can add extra, if desired. Obligatory table condiments include a small bowl of chopped onions and spicy vinegar, passed in a cruet.

Note: You may substitute a piece of smoked chicken, beef, or turkey, if you prefer.

SPICY VINEGAR

Makes 1 pint

This easy-to-prepare hot vinegar not only adds a bit of taste to mixed greens, it is also a wonderful gift for friends who cook. You will need a decorative pint bottle, sterilized, and a cork. You can sterilize the bottle by running it through the dishwasher.

1 carrot, peeled	1 small piece habanero or other
½-inch piece fresh ginger	hot chile, or to taste
3 cloves garlic, peeled but	4 sprigs fresh thyme
whole	1 pint cider vinegar

Cut the carrot into thin strips and place them in a sterilized 1-pint bottle. Force the ginger, garlic, chile, and thyme sprigs into the bottle. Add as much of the vinegar as will fit, cork, and let stand for 1 week. The intensity of the chile will increase over time.

HOLIDAY GINGERBREAD WITH MOLASSES WHIPPED CREAM

Serves 8

Gingerbread was a special-occasion treat for many of our ancestors. The molasses, a by-product of sugar production, was usually available and the spices were either received as gifts or "liberated" from the Big House kitchen. Many years ago, when this book first came out, I was making book-promotion rounds and visited Dr. Betty Shabazz's radio show with a sample for her to taste. I was astonished and delighted when after one bite, she smiled and said that hot-water gingerbread had been one of her husband, Malcolm X's, favorite treats and that she had prepared it for him frequently. Now, I think of her and of el Hadj Malik Shabazz (Malcolm X) whenever I make the dish.

1 tablespoon butter for the baking pan
1 cup molasses
½ cup boiling water
2¼ cups all-purpose flour
1 teaspoon baking soda
1½ teaspoons ground ginger

½ teaspoon ground cinnamon
½ teaspoon salt
4 tablespoons melted butter, melted
¼ cup packed dark brown sugar
Molasses Whipped Cream (recipe follows)

Preheat the oven to 350°F. Butter an 8-inch square baking pan.

In a heatproof medium bowl, combine the molasses and boiling water. Sift the flour, baking soda, ground ginger, cinnamon, and salt into the molasses mixture. Add the melted butter and brown sugar and beat well either by hand or with an electric mixer.

Pour the batter into the prepared pan. Bake until a toothpick inserted in the middle comes out clean, about 35 minutes. Allow to cool in the pan. Then cut into squares and serve with dollops of molasses whipped cream.

MOLASSES WHIPPED CREAM

Makes about 2 cups

This is a simple way to make whipped cream that adds a little something to anything it goes with. Later, I learned that there is an old Southern recipe for this khaki-hued deliciousness that is called Creole Fluff.

½ pint heavy whipping cream

3 tablespoons molasses

In a medium bowl, whisk the cream with a wire whisk, slowly drizzling the molasses into the cream. Whisk until the cream is whipped into firm peaks. (Alternatively, you can use an electric mixer.)

EGGNOG

Serves 6

This version of the classic holiday drink is a nonalcoholic one that can be savored by young and old alike. This eggnog is super rich and not for the dieter or the lactose intolerant. If there are concerns about salmonella-contaminated eggs, forego this recipe and use a commercially processed eggnog instead. For a more adult version, add brandy, rum, sherry, or port to taste.

5 large eggs, separated
¼ cup packed light brown
  sugar
3 cups half-and-half, well chilled
1 cup whole milk, well chilled
1 teaspoon vanilla extract

⅛ teaspoon freshly grated nutmeg,
  plus more for garnish
Pinch of ground cinnamon
¼ cup granulated sugar
Brandy, rum, sherry, or port
  (optional)

In a medium bowl, beat together the egg yolks and brown sugar. Slowly add the half-and-half, milk, vanilla, nutmeg, and cinnamon and whip until the mixture becomes foamy.

In an unlined copper bowl, combine the granulated sugar and egg whites and beat with a mixer or a whisk until they form soft peaks.

Slowly fold the egg whites into the milk mixture. Cover the eggnog and chill it until ready to serve. Add the alcohol of choice, if you wish.

The eggnog is traditionally served in small glass punch cups and is spiced up with the addition of a fresh grinding of nutmeg on the top of each cup.

PROJECT: SPICY VINEGAR GIFT BOTTLES

Starting out with a goal and accomplishing it is a thrill for all of us. It's actually one of the things that makes cooking so much fun: You get to see the end product of your labor in a reasonable amount of time and you get to enjoy it with family and friends. Setting goals and accomplishing them is one thing that gives us all a sense of purpose.

The project for this, the fifth night of Kwanzaa, is a cooking project that can be done by the whole family: the preparation of gift bottles of spicy vinegar to be given to family and friends. You can use fancy decorative bottles that can be purchased at kitchen supply or discount stores, or recycle wine or other attractive household bottles that have been scrupulously cleaned and scalded. The recipe for the spicy vinegar that appears on page 130 is simple and all hands in the household can participate. It is easily expanded: Simply purchase a gallon jug of inexpensive vinegar, get more of the other ingredients, and go to it. Even if children of the house are too small to wield a knife, they can scrape carrots, peel garlic, or simply stuff the carrot pieces into the narrow bottle necks with a chopstick or tiny fingers.

When the vinegar is finished, think of ways to decorate the bottles. Hardware stores and gourmet shops sell corks, and the season makes finding things like ribbon and fancy twine a snap. You may even wish to finish the bottle off with sealing wax and a handwritten label. You set a goal. You worked toward it. You attained it. Enjoy it. That's what Nia is all about.

FAMILY PAGE

....

....

....

....

....

....

....

....

....

....

....

....

....

....

....

....

THE SIXTH NIGHT

KUUMBA
(CREATIVITY)

THE KARAMU FEAST
A BLACK AMERICAN HEALING SUPPER

to do always as much as we can, in the way
we can, in order to leave our community more
beautiful and beneficial than we inherited it

Do well today on account of tomorrow.
—**Traditional saying**

At old revival meetings, preachers would lean over the pulpit and holler, "We need a healing here tonight." Indeed, in our communities, in our families, in our relationships, and in ourselves, we need a healing. I've taken the sixth night of Kwanzaa, the night of Kuumba, or creativity, to attempt to begin that process with a communal meal that opens the gates of remembrance through food and speaks of our history, our past, and our hopes for the future. I call it a healing supper. The format is loosely based on the Jewish Haggadah that accompanies the Passover feast and celebrates the Jewish peoples getting out of bondage in Egypt. The supper can be moved to any night of Kwanzaa, or indeed to any other time of the year that you, your family, or your community feels the need for a healing. The healing supper is designed to take us back over the centuries in remembrance of our journey that began in sorrow and ends with a vision of a new day. We can do this seated around our tables at home or anywhere we can gather together to share a meal in remembrance and celebration.

Our tables have traditionally been among our preferred places for communion, so what better place to begin the healing process? At our tables, generations speak with each other over platters of fried chicken and bowls of potato salad. Crisis-torn families are slowly knit back together while savoring slow-cooked greens or string beans and munching on cornbread. Dishes are passed, conversation begins, and a healing takes place. We need that healing now, as much as we did when I first wrote this in 1995, almost thirty years ago. Whether in a small family gathering around a simple scarred kitchen table that has served generations, or in a community-wide celebration complete with drummers and dignitaries, elders, and honored guests, the feast of Karamu that marks the sixth day of the holiday is the ideal time for us to come together to begin to take steps to heal ourselves.

In preparing the table and the foods for the Karamu Healing Supper, the principles of Ujamaa and Kuumba should be uppermost. Make a vow to try to use Black American purveyors. You don't have to spend a lot of money, but when you do spend, spread your cash around among our own folk. Seek out specialty merchants who sell African fabric to use as tablecloths. Think of using a Gullah basket or other representation of our creativity for your centerpiece. You may want to splurge on a dish or two from a local potter. Be inventive. Be creative. Be expressive. Be yourself. Make the table itself a celebration of your family and its creativity.

During the healing supper, the table is set with plates and silverware for the assembled guests. The *kikombe cha umoja* or communal chalice is set at the place of the elder who will lead the ceremony and pour libation. At each place, there should be a glass for wine, fruit juice, or Molasses Water (page 158), so that each guest will have a glass for the four libation sips that follow the reading of the opening statement and with which to propose toasts and offer humorous interventions throughout the meal. The healing supper is about the celebration of how we got here, how we survived, and where we hope that we're going. Table conversation, toasts, and comments should be a way to share experiences, share the pains, share the laughter, share the joy. Tall tales, family stories, and jokes all have their place. They are all a part of our communal oral tradition. While this is not the time for *The Signifying Monkey* or off-color jokes; it is the time to remember, to retell, and to reminisce.

In addition to standard table settings, somewhere on the table there should be small bowls of the gel from the aloe plant, molasses, and sesame, as they will be referred to during the healing supper. When each is mentioned, the small bowl is passed and each guest dips in a finger to taste. An extra place is set symbolically at the communal table, with a plate of food, for all of those who went before whose names we do not know.

If possible, all of the guests should sit at one table. No "children's tables," please. The children are part of the reason for the healing supper and, along with the elders, are important and honored guests.

KWANZAA STATEMENT

As on all other nights of the holiday, the ceremony begins with the Kwanzaa question *Habari gani?* Tonight's response is *Kuumba*. The response is followed by the lighting of the Kwanzaa candles on the *kinara*, tonight the last red candle, that of Kuumba, or creativity. All should stand as a sign of respect during the lighting of the candles and the pouring of the libation. At the beginning of the meal, the libation is poured and the names of the known deceased members of the host family are called while an elder who has been selected to lead the group says:

Light, peace, progress, and evolution to the ancestors of the _____ family.

Light, peace, progress, and evolution to the ancestors of those assembled here.

Light, peace, progress, and evolution to the ancestors of all people of color throughout the world.

Light, peace, progress, and evolution to those who symbolize the principle of Kuumba, creativity, particularly to those spirits from Africa and this hemisphere who kept us keepin' on with their stories and songs, their music and laughter, their dance, design, and dedication.

Tonight, and all nights of the year, we celebrate the artistry of our people: the griots and the bricklayers, the office workers and opera singers, cooks and carpenters, poets and politicians, inventors and quiltmakers, rappers and wordsmiths, doctors, deacons, and dressmakers—in short all of those who with their inventiveness and their creativity enabled us to survive by daily making our communities, and indeed the larger community of the world, a better and more beautiful place.

OPENING HEALING SUPPER STATEMENT

After the candles have been lighted, the libation has been poured, and all have been seated, the youngest person present begins the Healing Ceremony.

YOUNGEST PERSON: *If we forget our past, we will be doomed to repeat it.*

ELDER: *From too much sleeping we have forgotten.*

ALL: *We awaken to the knowledge of the past and the promise of the future. We awaken and we remember. (All take a sip from their glasses.)*

ELDER: *We are the descendants of the peoples of Africa. The grasslands and the forest, the Sahel and the seashore come together in us.*

ALL: *We salute our African past. (Sip from glasses.)*

ELDER: *We are the descendants of the peoples of the Americas: Creek and Cherokee, Seminole and Wampanoag, Choctaw and Sioux, Caribe and Quisqueya and Garifuna come together in us. Even if we do not have their blood in our veins, we walk on their land, and so we honor them.*

ALL: *We salute our Native American past. (Sip from glasses.)*

ELDER: *We are children of a new place. Never before in the history of the world have there been any like us. The blood of all nations is in us. We cover north, south, east, and west. The blood of the world runs in us.*

ALL: *We salute our international past. (Sip from glasses.)*

ELDER: *Tonight, as we sit around this table and share this meal, we take a journey back over time and space. We take this journey to trace and remember one made by our ancestors who were kidnapped and brought to this land in bondage. It is a journey that begins in sorrow and ends this evening with the* *vision of a new day. We take this journey to link us with our past. We take this journey to remember, so that all of us seated at this table and all tables like this will know our past and remember, so that we can determine our future. We take this symbolic journey tonight so that in the future we will all truly be free.*

Following the preliminary statement, the food is passed. Food is served family-style. Elders should help youngsters, and all should help those who can't help themselves, symbolizing the need to aid each other within our communities.

The appetizer course includes pickled black-eyed peas. As that dish is passed, the first honored guest reads.

GUEST #1: *In the beginning, we were African: Wolof and Tutsi, Mandinka and Hausa, Ewe and Yoruba, Ashanti and Luba, Fulani and Kongo. In our African homelands, we ate many things. We eat black-eyed peas tonight to remind us of the peas and beans that we ate in that other place. We eat them for luck and for wisdom and to remind us where we are from.*

After the course is finished, there is a minute of silence, after which the first honored guest continues to read.

GUEST #1: *We were captured and taken against our will, sent forth from ports like Gorée and Kormantine, Ouidah and Elmina, Calabar, and Cape Coast, Luanda and Benguela. Our names were taken from us and our heritage mocked. Our strength survived.*

ALL: *We honor the survival of our ancestors.*

The fish course is served. As the dish is passed, the next honored guest reads.

GUEST #2: *The water deep. The water wide. The water profound. There is mystery in the water. There is another Africa at the bottom of the ocean peopled with the spirits of those who did not survive the journey. Others used water to take us away from our home and it is the water that will take us back home. We salute the water mother that is the source of all life. She gives us her fish to eat. We eat them and rejoice, knowing that she helped us survive. Tonight we eat fish as a symbol of our survival.*

After the course is finished, there is a minute of silence, during which the second honored guest reads.

GUEST #2: *May the spirits of those who live under the water guide us and heal us. May they help us to honor the sacrifice they made in everything we do. (The small bowl with aloe gel is passed and all guests dip in a finger and taste the bitterness.) We taste this bitter aloe to remind us of the trials of our ancestors.*

ALL: *We remember the African homeland of our ancestors.*

The turkey with stuffing is served. As the dish is served, the cook who prepared the turkey reads.

COOK: *We were brought to another land. In this new land, we met new foods. Among these new foods was turkey. The way we prepare a turkey speaks to who we are. Recipes for stuffings are handed down in families and are a part of our heritage in this land. Tonight, we eat my family's recipe for _____ stuffing. I learned it from _____ and serve it to you tonight. Eat and share my history.*

VEGETARIAN ALTERNATIVE

Many of us are becoming vegetarian. If that is the case with your family and friends, you can present a vegetarian casserole at this point and have the cook discuss it saying:

> COOK: *We were brought to another land. In this land we met new foods. In our family we have decided to leave behind the eating of meat and to eat in a vegetarian manner. This speaks to who we are and to who we hope our children will become. Our recipe for _____ is a family one, one that we have developed and one that we savor. I learned it from _____ and serve it to you tonight. Eat and enjoy my history.*

There should be many vegetables, but there should always be dishes of stewed okra, baked tomatoes, and white rice, as well as cornbread, as these foods will be referred to. As the okra, tomatoes, and rice are passed, the next honored guest reads.

GUEST #3: *We ate okra in our African Motherland. We brought it to this land. We eat okra tonight to celebrate our links with our past.*

We eat tomatoes and cornbread tonight to symbolize our links with our new land that gave us these foods and with the people who first walked here.

We eat rice tonight to symbolize the work of those who built this country, who went unheralded, unpaid, and unsung. In eating rice, we salute their genius, their work, and their strength.

The meal is served and savored. When it is over, there is a minute of silence, after which the small dish of molasses is passed around and the third honored guest reads.

GUEST #3: *We taste molasses tonight to symbolize the work of our ancestors in this land they worked to create who built, and plowed, and harvested. In tasting this molasses, we honor their memory.*

ALL: *We honor the memory of our American ancestors.*

The dessert is served. During the service the next guest to the right reads.

GUEST #4: *A life without sweetness is a life without hope. We eat this dessert tonight to remind ourselves that all life needs sweetening. We eat this dessert tonight to remind ourselves of our reasons for living, of the joys of family, of the delights of friendship, of the comforts of hearth and home, and of our sweet hopes for the generations yet to come.*

ALL: *We celebrate the sweetness of life.*

At the conclusion of the meal, the fifth honored guest signals the end of the meal by passing around the small bowl of sesame seeds.

GUEST #5: *May the joys of all of our people be as numerous as the seeds in this bowl. May we grow and thrive in the year to come. May we honor the principles of the Nguzo Saba throughout the year as we do throughout Kwanzaa, and may we work together to heal, unite, and advance our people and ourselves.*

ALL: *May we work together to heal, unite, and advance ourselves and all peoples.*

THE KARAMU FEAST

A Black American Healing Supper

Appetizer
Pickled Black-Eyed Peas (page 147)

Fish Course
Biokosso (page 148)

Main Dish
Turkey with Heritage Stuffing or Vegetarian Casserole (page 149)

Vegetables
Steamed Okra (page 152)

Baked Tomatoes (page 153)

Plain White Rice (page 60)

Bread
Herbed Cornbread (page 154)

Condiment
Spicy Cranberry Chutney (page 155)

Salad
Red Leaf Lettuce with Clementines (page 156)

Dessert
Pecan Pie with Molasses Whipped Cream (page 157)

Beverage
Rum, wine, fruit juice, or Molasses Water (page 158)

PICKLED BLACK-EYED PEAS

Serves 8

Black-eyed peas are a part of our African legacy. In this recipe they are marinated with vinegar and hot chile to create a savory dish that is also known as Texas Caviar. The black-eyed peas can be eaten as a condiment or a side dish. Here, they are served in a lettuce cup as an appetizer. To save time during the busy holiday, this recipe calls for canned black-eyed peas, though the dish can also be made with fresh or frozen peas. It takes on a festive air with the addition of dark purple, red, and green bell pepper replicating the colors of the candles in the *kinara*. Note that the black-eyed peas must marinate overnight.

2 (16-ounce) cans black-eyed peas, well drained

¼ cup minced dark purple bell pepper

¼ cup minced red bell pepper

¼ cup minced green bell pepper

1 small onion, minced

1 tablespoon finely minced garlic

2 tablespoons red wine vinegar

1 tablespoon balsamic vinegar

⅓ cup olive oil

2 sprigs fresh thyme, leaves picked

1 head Boston lettuce, separated into 8 leaves

In a medium bowl, combine the black-eyed peas, bell peppers, onion, and garlic. In another bowl, whisk together both vinegars, the olive oil, and thyme. Pour the marinade over the black-eyed pea mixture, cover with plastic wrap, and refrigerate overnight so that the flavors blend, stirring occasionally.

When ready to serve, place the lettuce leaves on individual plates, spoon the black-eyed peas onto the lettuce, and serve.

BIOKOSSO

Serves 8

This dish comes from the southern Côte d'Ivoire, where a version is prepared using a banana leaf wrapper. Here aluminum foil provides a reliable and readily available substitute. Select small fish of even size so that they will all cook in the same amount of time.

7 large firm-ripe tomatoes, seeded, and coarsely chopped

2 large onions, chopped

2 cloves garlic, chopped

1 teaspoon minced habanero or other hot chile, or to taste

2 teaspoons fresh lemon juice

Salt and freshly ground black pepper

8 medium butterfish or small snappers, scaled and gutted, with heads left on

In a food processor or blender, combine the tomatoes, onions, garlic, chile, lemon juice, and salt and pepper to taste and pulse until the mixture is transformed into a thick, coarse paste.

Tear off 8 sheets of aluminum foil large enough to enclose the fish. For each packed, dab a heaping spoonful of the paste onto the foil, add the fish, then an additional heaping spoonful of the paste. Close the foil into a packet and crimp it shut with your fingers.

Preheat the broiler.

When ready, place the packets of foil on the broiler rack and broil until the fish is cooked, about 7 to 10 minutes.

Serve warm in the packets. Guests will unfold the foil on their plates.

TURKEY WITH HERITAGE STUFFING OR VEGETARIAN CASSEROLE

These pages are blank so that you can write down your family recipe for turkey and stuffing or your vegetarian specialty. If you're not sure, ask your mama or dad, grandma or grandad, aunts and uncles.

No family recipe? That's too bad, but here's the place to start a tradition. Ask around. Check the papers, the magazines, and the cookbooks and find an appealing recipe for turkey and stuffing or a vegetarian casserole. (They aren't hard to find at this time of year.) Try it, and if you truly love it and think it passes the audition, write it in after the holidays. (Don't hurry; give it time to take on some of your additions and subtractions.) Then start your own tradition.

FAMILY PAGES

....

....

....

....

....

....

....

....

....

....

....

....

....

....

FAMILY PAGES

STEAMED OKRA

Serves 8

Many folks just don't seem to like okra. However, the green pod that is a relative of both cotton and the hibiscus is a part of our culinary history. By now, it's no secret that okra originated in Africa, and most of the more inventive recipes using it come from the African diaspora, where it turns up fried, boiled, steamed, sautéed, and blanched in soups, and in salads. This dish is for purists. The smallest, most tender okra pods are cooked until done in a bit of water. A dash of lemon juice is added at the last minute to cut some of the "sliminess" that offends some people.

2 pounds small okra pods

2 teaspoons fresh lemon juice

Cut off the fibrous stem ends of the okra.

In a medium saucepan, bring 2 cups water a rolling boil. Add the okra, reduce the heat, cover, and cook until the okra is firm but fork-tender, 5 to 6 minutes. Add the lemon juice for the last 2 minutes of cooking time. Drain and serve warm.

BAKED TOMATOES

Serves 8

Tomatoes are one of the food gifts that the American hemisphere gave to the world. They traveled from the Americas to Africa, where they became a treasured part of the continent's cooking. Interestingly, there is some discussion that tomatoes might have finally reached the northeastern United States via people of African descent from the Caribbean. However they arrived, they're a welcome addition to our culinary repertoire. Here they're simply cored, seasoned, and baked along with the turkey. If you're doing a vegetarian meal, just cook them in a baking dish.

8 large firm-ripe tomatoes
Salt and freshly ground black pepper

Herbs from heritage stuffing (optional)

Preheat the oven to 350 degrees F.

Core the tomatoes and sprinkle them with salt and freshly ground black pepper. (If making turkey with stuffing, you might want to add some of the herbs and seasonings so that the tastes will harmonize.) Place the tomatoes in a baking dish and bake until soft and juicy, about 20 minutes.

Note: If you are cooking the tomatoes while the turkey is roasting, add them around the turkey pan (where they can absorb the drippings) in the last 20 minutes of cooking. If making a vegetarian casserole, just cook them by themselves.

HERBED CORNBREAD

Makes 16 pieces

Like tomatoes, corn and cornmeal are new additions to the traditional African diet. However, they are additions that have been so gleefully adopted that it is virtually impossible to think of the cooking of the African Atlantic world without them. This cornbread uses frozen corn (let's be realistic about what most fresh corn tastes like at this time of the year), a hint of jalapeño chiles, and a bit of thyme for seasoning.

Softened butter for the pan
¾ cup yellow cornmeal
¾ cup all-purpose flour
2 tablespoons sugar
1 tablespoon baking powder
½ teaspoon salt
1 teaspoon dried thyme, crumbled
¾ cup milk

2 teaspoons minced pickled jalapeño or other minced hot chile, or to taste
1 large egg
3 tablespoons butter, melted
2 tablespoons coarsely chopped thawed frozen corn kernels, well drained

Preheat the oven to 425°F. Butter an 8-inch square baking pan.

Sift the cornmeal, flour, sugar, baking powder, and salt into a large bowl. Add the thyme, milk, chile, egg, and melted butter and beat for 1 minute or stir until the mixture is smooth. Add the corn, stirring well to make sure that the pieces are well distributed throughout the batter.

Pour the batter into the prepared pan. Bake until the top is lightly browned and a toothpick inserted into the middle comes out clean, about 20 minutes.

Cut into squares and serve hot.

SPICY CRANBERRY CHUTNEY

Makes 1½ cups

Cranberry sauce of some kind just seems to be a must with turkey and stuffing. However, the whole cranberry or jellied sauce that comes in a can sometimes just doesn't have enough zing to set off a well-cooked turkey properly and to complement the well-seasoned tastes of our food. Here, then, is a cranberry chutney that I've been playing around with. See if it works as well with your turkey and heritage stuffing.

1½ cups cranberries, fresh or frozen (see Note)

1-inch piece fresh ginger, scraped

1 clove garlic, minced

2 teaspoons minced orange zest

1 teaspoon minced pickled jalapeño chile, or to taste

½ cup fresh lemon juice

⅓ cup sugar

In a food processor or blender, combine the cranberries, ginger, garlic, orange zest, and chile and pulse until you have a grainy paste. (You may have to add a bit of the lemon juice to get it going.)

Spoon the mixture into a nonreactive medium saucepan. Add the lemon juice and sugar, stirring well to make sure that all of the ingredients are evenly distributed. Bring to a boil over medium heat, then reduce the heat and continue to cook, stirring occasionally, until the chutney reaches a jamlike consistency, about 25 minutes. Stir all the way to the bottom of the saucepan to be sure that the mixture is not sticking to the bottom and scorching.

The chutney can be prepared a week or so ahead, in which case, pour it into a sterilized jar and refrigerate until ready to use. If making it the same day, allow it to cool to room temperature and spoon it into a serving dish.

Note: Frozen cranberries can be used straight from the freezer.

RED LEAF LETTUCE WITH CLEMENTINES

Serves 8

Clementines are small tangerine-like fruits that are available during the holiday season. The ones from Morocco are slightly tarter than those from Spain, and just perfect for this salad. Their juice turns up in the dressing.

1 large head red leaf lettuce

6 clementines, peeled

½ cup pomegranate seeds

1 teaspoon finely minced garlic

Pomegranate Tangerine Dressing (recipe follows)

Wash the lettuce, dry the leaves on absorbent paper, and place them in a large glass salad bowl.

With a sharp knife, remove the membrane from the clementine segments and seed them. Add the clementine segments to the salad. Add the pomegranate seeds and garlic. Toss the salad and drizzle on the dressing.

POMEGRANATE TANGERINE DRESSING

Makes about ½ cup

½ cup pomegranate seeds

2 tablespoons fresh tangerine juice

2 tablespoons olive oil

2 tablespoons balsamic vinegar

Pinch of sugar

Place the pomegranate seeds in a sieve. Place the sieve over a bowl and press the juice from the seeds with the back of a wooden spoon or a wooden potato masher. Reserve 2 tablespoons and enjoy the rest. Place the pomegranate juice and tangerine juice in a small bowl. Add the olive oil, vinegar, and sugar and whisk thoroughly. Taste and adjust the seasonings. Cover with plastic wrap and refrigerate for 1 hour before using.

PECAN PIE WITH MOLASSES WHIPPED CREAM

Serves 8

Pecans are a part of our Southern roots. Here, with the addition of a bit of molasses and brown sugar, they are transformed into a rich pecan pie that brings a taste of sweetness to end the meal.

Basic Pie Dough (page 86)

3 large eggs

⅓ cup packed light brown sugar

⅓ cup granulated sugar

Pinch of salt

⅓ cup butter, melted

¾ cup dark corn syrup

¼ cup light molasses

1 cup broken pecans

¼ cup pecan halves

2 cups Molasses Whipped Cream
  (page 132)

Preheat the oven to 375°F.

Roll out the pie dough and fit it into a 9-inch pie plate, fluting the edges. Cover the center of the pie shell with a sheet of aluminum foil, weight it with dried peas or beans, and bake it for 15 minutes or until set. Remove from the oven, but leave the oven on lowering the heat to 350°F.

In a medium bowl, briskly stir together the eggs, both sugars, the salt, melted butter, corn syrup, and molasses until they are well mixed. Stir in the broken pecans.

Remove the foil and the beans from the pie shell and arrange the pecan halves in the bottom of the shell. Carefully pour the egg mixture into the pie shell.

Place in the oven and until the crust is golden brown and the filling is set, about 45 minutes.

Serve warm, topped with molasses whipped cream.

MOLASSES WATER

Makes 1 quart

During the period of many of our ancestors' American enslavement, water was their only beverage. For holidays and special occasions, they improvised, using the only sweetener that they had: molasses. I've taken liberties with history and added a sprig of fresh mint and a squeeze of fresh lemon juice.

1 quart water
½ cup molasses, or to
  taste
¼ cup fresh lemon juice

5 sprigs fresh mint
Ice
Mint sprigs and lemon slices, for
  garnish

In a container, stir together the water, molasses, and lemon juice, stirring thoroughly to make sure that the molasses is well mixed in. Refrigerate for at least 2 hours or until well chilled.

When ready to serve, bruise the mint by pressing it against the side of a serving pitcher with the bowl of a spoon, add ice, and pour in the molasses water. Serve chilled in glasses decorated with fresh mint sprigs and thin slices of lemon for garnish.

PROJECT: HEALING SUPPER CEREMONY

THE PROJECT FOR THIS, the sixth night of Kwanzaa, the night of Kuumba, is to make the text of the healing supper ceremony (page 141) available for all of the guests. The pages can be decorated with pictures of people in the African Atlantic world who represent the virtues of Kuumba, with designs representing the Nguzo Saba, or with any other design that your family or organization feels is appropriate to the purpose of your healing supper. Let loose your inner artist and use the principle of Kuumba (creativity), to which this night is dedicated.

FAMILY PAGES

FAMILY PAGES

....
....
....
....
....
....
....
....
....
....
....
....
....
....

THE SEVENTH NIGHT

IMANI

(FAITH)

to believe with all our hearts in our people,
our parents, our teachers, our leaders, and
the righteousness and victory of our struggle

*The African race is like a rubber ball; the harder you
knock it to the ground, the higher it will rise.*
—Traditional saying

On the seventh and final night of Kwanzaa, as on all other nights of the holiday, the celebration begins with the question *Habari gani?* Tonight's answer is *Imani*, or faith. The asking of the Kwanzaa question is followed by the pouring of the libation from the *kikombe cha umoja* and the lighting of the candles of the *kinara*. Tonight the last candle, the green candle of Imani, is lighted. After the candles are lighted, thoughts turn to the spirits of those who represented the virtues of Imani in our communities.

Tonight is the night we celebrate the spirit of Imani (faith).

Tonight, and all other nights of the year, we celebrate the spirits of those who have gone before who represent the values of Imani.

We celebrate the spirits of:
    Amenhotep IV of Egypt
    Agõime of Brazil
    Robert Nesta Marley of Jamaica
    Ben Ali Mohamet
    The Candomblé Tradition of Brazil
    _____ (your family selection[s])

and all those who kept their bright light of faith burning despite obstacles and odds that would have driven lesser beings to give up, give in, and give over.

Tonight, and all nights, we celebrate the spirits of all of those who are here with us.

Tonight, and all nights, we celebrate the spirits of those who are yet to come.

On this, the final night of Kwanzaa, we dedicate ourselves to uphold the values of Imani and all of the principles of the Nguzo Saba. In the year that has just come in, we will have faith in the future, faith in our people, and faith in ourselves, that we may work to create a better world.

AMENHOTEP IV (AKHENATON) OF EGYPT
(PHARAOH, 1379–1362 BC)

Faith can move mountains, many of us were told while growing up. In ancient Egypt, Amenhotep's faith in the power of the physical sun changed the way that the world has looked at religion ever since. Was he a heretic, a religious fanatic, or a visionary? Even today, more than three thousand years after his reign from 1379 to 1362 BC, the question is still debated.

Born to kingship, Amenhotep IV ascended the throne in 1379 BC. Physically weak, he may have had a genetic abnormality. He ruled surrounded by an inner circle that consisted of his mother, Queen Ti; his wife, the beautiful Queen Nefertiti; and the husband of his childhood nurse, the priest Eye. Before Amenhotep IV's reign, the priests of Amon-Ra, the sun god, had attained primacy in Egypt and had become a powerful political force. Amenhotep IV would change all that. He openly challenged the priesthood and introduced the worship of Aton, the material sun, claiming that the new religion had been revealed to him; he reasoned that the sun was the source of life and heat and, through its rays, everywhere. Although other gods were tolerated, Aton became the single deity.

In witness to his devotion to the new faith, he changed his throne name from Amenhotep, which means "Amon is content," to Akhenaton (Ikhnaton), meaning "It is well with Aton." He also built many temples to the new god, including one in the midst of the temple to Amon-Ra. He had the names and images of Amon-Ra removed from all temples and tombs and moved the capital to Tell el-Amarna, a town he called Akhetaton. Akhenaton envisioned his new god as a beneficent god, one who was "father and mother of all he had made." It was revolutionary, but it was not to last.

Following the deaths of Akhenaton and Nefertiti, the old order returned, but

Akhenaton's notion of one supreme universal god would live on. We salute the spirit of Akhenaton tonight as that of a visionary, one who saw beyond the day-to-day. We honor him for his courage, his insights, and for taking the first steps in establishing a concept that would change the world.

AGÕTIME OF BRAZIL
(LATE EIGHTEENTH AND EARLY NINETEENTH CENTURIES)

No one is sure when Agõtime was born nor when she died. What we are sure of is that she lived. It is believed that she was born in the West African country of the Fongbè then known as Dan Homè now known as Benin toward the end of the eighteenth century. She is recorded as being one of the wives of King Agoglo of Dahomey who ruled from 1789, the year of the French Revolution, to 1797. When her husband died, she, unlike the childless wives who went to the grave with their husband, lived. She was passed on to Agoglo's first wife's son, Adādozā, and went to live in the precincts of the Panther Compound of the king's wives in Abomey.

After five years in the Panther Compound, she was perceived as a threat to the king's sovereignty and sold into slavery because she was related to Gakpe, who was also a pretender to the throne. Like so many others, she last set foot on the soil of the African coast outside of the Portuguese fort of São Jão Baptista de Ajuda, in the town known today as Ouidah. She was sent to Brazil where she, with the others aboard the ship, landed in the port city of Salvador da Bahia de Todos os Santos. Where she went and what happened to her from there is little known, but she surfaces again, enslaved, in São Luis de Maranhão on the northern coast of the country. Legend has it that Agõtime knew she was to be taken and sent away from her African home and that her oracles told her to take her gods with her. Evidently she did, for the city of São Luis de Maranhão today is known for the religion known as Tambor de Mina. There, and only there, the deities of the royal family of Abomey are venerated outside of Africa to this day.

The story does not end there, for in 1818, the saying, "Two suns cannot exist at the same time," was borne out. While the war drums played, Adādozā was relieved of the crown by Gakpe, who took the king name Ghezo. He ruled for forty years. Some say that he sent emissaries to Brazil in search of Agõtime and that she was returned to glory in his kingdom. Others say she wandered off into the Brazilian forests, never to be seen again. Whatever Agōtime's fate, we salute her tonight for embodying the virtue of Imani. Throughout her harrowing history, she never lost her faith ; she went from royalty to slave to priestess, taking her faith with her, nurturing it, and then leaving it behind as a legacy so that the world would remember.

ROBERT NESTA MARLEY OF JAMAICA
(1945–1981)

In his short life Robert Nesta Marley not only made his mark on the international music world, he was also a profound influence on the people of his country and on the minds of the world. Born in poverty in Rhoden Hall in St. Ann, Jamaica, in 1945 and seasoned in Kingston's notorious Trench Town neighborhood, Marley articulated the cry of Jamaica's underclass in his music. During his brief career, first with the Wailers, then solo, he became the voice of rebellion for all people who don't have what they want. When he sang, "Them Belly Full (But We Hungry)," he spoke for all people who are made beggars at the feast. "Buffalo Soldiers" expressed his solidarity in the struggle with Black Americans from the United States and "Redemption Song" speaks of a never-ending will to survive.

Marley's importance, though, extends far beyond his music to his life and his personal philosophy, which was informed by his Rastafarian faith, a gentle doctrine that asks all men to live in peace. His faith in his religion and in his people made him work to ensure harmony in his country. It also helped him see beyond the conflict to the notion that all should live in peace and that the earth provides enough for all of us. We salute the spirit of Robert Nesta "Bob" Marley tonight for teaching us gentleness. We remember him for his admonition to "Get Up! Stand Up! Don't Give Up the Fight." Finally, we honor the spirit of Bob Marley tonight for bringing us joy from sorrow, music from hardship, for his "Positive Vibration," and for reminding us that where the light of faith burns bright, nothing is impossible.

BEN ALI MOHAMET
(NINETEENTH CENTURY)

No one knows very much about Ben Ali Mohamet, better known as Bilali Mohamet, but it is thought that he was brought to the plantation of a man named Thomas Spaulding on Sapelo Island, Georgia, from Nassau in the Bahamas. Because he is said to have spoken French, there are those who believe that before living in Nassau, he had been enslaved somewhere in the French-speaking West Indies.

Bilali Mohamet was different from the other Black people of his area. In fact, he distinguished himself so much that others recalled him and his ways in their oral witness to the trials of slavery. These testimonies reveal that Bilali Mohamet was a man who ate food that was prepared differently from that of the others. He prostrated himself to pray at sunup and sundown, and he wore a fezlike cap. He had many children and they, too, were different. They had names like Bintu, Medina, and Fatima.

Nothing much else survived about Bilali except in the memories of his descendants and those who knew him, until the Georgia State Library received a document in 1930 that was thought to be his journal, written in what seemed to be Arabic. Perplexed, they attempted to decipher the text to no avail. Finally, after the text had been taken to African Islamic scholars, a discovery was made. The work that Ben Ali Mohamet had written was his transcription of the Risala, a legal text written by abu Muhammed 'abdullah ben 'abi Zaid of Kairouan, the Islamic university town in what is today Tunisia. In particular, Mohamet had transcribed the introduction and sections dealing with ablutions and the call to prayer. The confusion came because, like others taken from Africa, Ben Ali Mohamet took with him only what he had stored in his mind; he had transcribed the text from memory, the memory of a young African Koranic student decades earlier. What better testimony to the power of Imani (faith)!

Tonight, on this final night of Kwanzaa, we salute the spirit of Ben Ali Mohamet for his unswerving faith, for his persistence and perseverance despite overwhelming odds. We salute his will to survive and to maintain his traditions. We look at his achievements, know the adversity under which he accomplished them, and learn that with faith all things are possible.

THE CANDOMBLÉ TRADITION OF BRAZIL

On this final night of Kwanzaa, instead of selecting an individual to honor, the choice is a religious tradition: Candomblé. Candomblé is an African diasporic religious practice that is a Brazilian example of those that descended from the New World traditions of a mix of peoples of western and central Africa. Candomblé which originated among the enslaved people of the Brazilian state of Bahia in the late eighteenth or early nineteenth century, is based on the celebration and veneration of forces of nature and deified ancestors. It has been described by practitioners as one of the world's early ecological religions for its acknowledgment and valorization of people's connection to nature.

Unlike many world faiths, Candomblé does not send out missionaries to develop new converts. There are no street corner proselytizers. Rather, individuals find the practice as a part of their life's journey and are brought to it by a crisis, need, or desire. If they become members of a specific and autonomous *terreiro* and follow its initiatory practices, they become a part of the Candomblé religious community at large.

Candomblé, though, is more than an ecological religion; many also find it to be a faith of exceptional acceptance and tolerance as investigated in recent works like *Queering Black Atlantic Religions* by Roberto Strongman. Many of the *terreiros* have been welcoming to members of the LGBTQ+ community since inception, and some of the notable leaders of the religion have been LGBTQ+ themselves.

On this evening of Imani, we honor Candomblé because it reminds us to value the earth on which we live and the land and water on which we depend. We honor Candomblé as a religion that also reminds us that tolerance and acceptance are virtues that we all should strive for, no matter what our faith.

Our acknowledgment of the need to be good stewards of the land and to honor all who walk on it is a fitting way to end tonight's celebration and the year's Kwanzaa season.

The menu celebrating Imani is a meal focused on where we're from and where we're heading, and features thoughtful foods, foods for thought, and some classics to bring in the New Year.

Appetizer
Dates, Figs, and Milk (page 175)

Soup
Fruit Soup (page 176)

Salad
North African Carrot Salad (page 177)

Main Dish
Red Snapper Fillets in Creole Court Bouillon (page 178)

Starch
Plain White Rice (page 60)

Suggested Vegetables
Hoppin' John and Greens (page 180)

Southern Succotash (page 183)

Dessert
Carrot Cake (page 184)

Beverage
Raspberry Orange Bubbly (page 185)

DATES, FIGS, AND MILK

Serves 8

There is lowercase faith and capital letter Faith. This menu begins with a minute for capital letter Faith. Many celebrants of Kwanzaa spend the week fasting during daylight hours as a sign of their commitment to the Nguzo Saba. For them, and for the faith (both small and capital letters) of our ancestors, this meal begins with a symbolic fast-breaking dish of dates, figs, and milk. Nibble on the fruit and sip the milk while remembering those whose faith and Faith brought you through.

1 pound Medjool dates

1 pound dried or fresh Smyrna figs

Almonds or other nuts (optional)

1 quart milk of choice (see Note)

Arrange the dates and figs on a platter. You may wish to add some almonds or other nuts. The platter is circulated around the table with each diner taking a few. The milk is poured into small glasses from a pitcher while the family thinks about the Nguzo Saba of Imani.

Note: Those who are lactose intolerant may wish to participate with a glass of cool water.

FRUIT SOUP

Serves 8

This is a soup of hot winter fruit juices that my mother dreamed up to serve as the beginning of fancy meals. Fruit soup can be prepared from fresh (I prefer fresh) or canned juices, but select the best, whichever variety you choose, because the quality of the soup will depend on the quality of the juice. You can also vary the taste by using other juices that you have available. (But be careful; apple juice will make everything else brown!)

2 cups white grape juice

2 cups passion fruit juice

2 cups fresh orange juice

1 cup fresh grapefruit juice

1 cup fresh tangerine juice

1 tablespoon fresh lemon juice

1 cup water

½ teaspoon ground cinnamon

1 teaspoon freshly grated
   nutmeg

8 thin orange slices and freshly
   grated nutmeg, for garnish

In a saucepan, combine the juices, the water, cinnamon, and nutmeg and bring to a boil, stirring occasionally. Ladle into soup bowls and garnish each one with a slice of orange and a grating of nutmeg.

NORTH AFRICAN CARROT SALAD

Serves 6 to 8

The light, healthy salads of North Africa remind us that in the upcoming year, vegetables should be more of a part of our lives. Here, cooked carrots are spiced with a pinch of cinnamon and powdered sugar and seasoned with orange juice and orange flower water.

1½ pounds carrots, peeled and
  cut into ½-inch rounds
¼ cup fresh orange juice
1 tablespoon fresh lemon
  juice

½ teaspoon freshly ground
  cinnamon (see Note)
1 teaspoon powdered sugar
1 tablespoon orange flower water,
  or to taste
Fresh mint sprigs, for garnish

Bring a saucepan of water to a boil. Add the carrots and cook until they are fork-tender, 6 to 8 minutes.

Meanwhile, in a small bowl, stir together the orange juice and lemon juice. In another small bowl, mix the cinnamon with the powdered sugar.

When the carrots are cooked, drain them, place them in a glass salad bowl, and pour the juices over them. Refrigerate them for 1 hour.

When ready to serve, sprinkle them with the cinnamon-sugar and drizzle the orange flower water over them. Serve garnished with mint sprigs.

Note: Grind the cinnamon using a mortar and pestle or a coffee grinder you reserve for spices.

RED SNAPPER FILLETS IN CREOLE COURT BOUILLON

Serves 4 to 6

This is a variation on the redfish court bouillon that is traditionally served in many of the Black Creole homes of New Orleans at Christmastime. Here, though, instead of the entire baked fish, snapper fillets are poached in the Creole court bouillon, which is more like a Creole sauce than like the classic French court bouillon poaching liquid. You may wish to serve this as a main dish, or as an alternative main dish along with the more traditional roasts that usually appear on the New Year table.

1 tablespoon olive oil

2 tablespoons all-purpose flour

1 teaspoon finely crushed allspice berries

1 teaspoon minced fresh thyme

1 medium onion, minced

1 clove garlic, minced

1 tablespoon minced celery

2 tablespoons minced green bell pepper

1 tablespoon minced scallion

1 tablespoon minced fresh parsley

2 bay leaves

8 large tomatoes, peeled, seeded, and coarsely chopped

2 cups water

½ cup dry white wine

8 red snapper fillets (4 ounces each)

2 tablespoons fresh lemon juice

¼ teaspoon minced hot chile, or to taste

Salt

Plain White Rice (page 60)

In a large heavy nonreactive skillet, heat the olive oil over low heat. Slowly sprinkle in the flour and cook, stirring constantly until you have a tan paste (the roux). Add the allspice, thyme, onion, garlic, celery, bell pepper, scallion, parsley, bay leaves, tomatoes, water, and wine and bring the mixture slowly to a boil over medium eat, stirring constantly, making sure that there are no lumps. The mixture will thicken into a heavy sauce.

Add the fish, reduce the heat to low, and simmer the mixture until the fish is cooked, about 5 minutes. Remove the fish fillets and keep them on a heated platter.

Add the lemon juice, chile, and salt to taste to the sauce, stir into the mixture well, and continue to cook for 3 minutes. Taste the sauce and adjust to taste.

Serve the sauce spooned over the fish fillets. Serve hot with rice.

HOPPIN' JOHN AND GREENS

The tradition in many of our families on New Year's Day is to eat Hoppin' John (some form of field peas and rice) for luck and greens to represent folding money during the incoming year. Far be it from me to tell you which peas to use—some use black-eyed peas, others lady peas or Sapelo red peas—or how to cook them. So here are some pages for you to use to write down your way with Hoppin' John and Greens. (If you don't have recipes, check online or in one of your Black American cookbooks.)

FAMILY PAGES

....

....

....

....

....

....

....

....

....

....

....

....

....

....

....

....

FAMILY PAGES

....

....

....

....

....

....

....

....

....

....

....

....

....

....

....

SOUTHERN SUCCOTASH

Serves 8

This dish of okra, corn, and tomatoes is a staple on my New Year table. It's simple to make and can even be prepared with little loss of flavor from frozen ingredients and canned tomatoes. The trick is to use a hot chile like a habanero or Scotch bonnet and spice it just enough so that your guests will say, "Ah!"

2 cups corn kernels, cut from the cob or frozen

½ pound fresh or frozen okra, topped, tailed, and cut into rounds

6 firm-ripe tomatoes, peeled, seeded, and coarsely chopped, or 2½ cups canned chopped tomatoes

1 tablespoon fresh lemon juice

1 habanero or other hot chile, left whole and pricked with a fork

Salt and freshly ground black pepper

In a medium saucepan, combine the corn, okra, tomatoes, lemon juice, chile, and salt and black pepper to taste. Add the chile, making sure that it is pricked so that it doesn't explode and make the dish too hot. Bring to a boil over medium heat, then reduce the heat to low and cook for 30 minutes. Taste as it cooks and remove the chile (and reserve) when the dish is hot enough for your taste.

Serve hot with the minced chile on the side for those who wish to add a bit more heat.

CARROT CAKE

Serves 6 to 8

The whir of juicers is heard in our neighborhoods more and more. If you've ever wondered what to do with all of that pulp, try this carrot cake recipe. It's a wonderful way to use the pulp that's left over after the carrots have been juiced (see Note).

Softened butter and flour for the loaf pan

8 medium to large carrots, peeled

2 small McIntosh apples, peeled

2 teaspoons baking powder

1½ cups all-purpose flour

1 teaspoon freshly grated nutmeg

½ teaspoon ground cinnamon

½ teaspoon salt

3 large eggs

1 cup packed dark brown sugar

½ cup granulated sugar

¾ cup vegetable oil

2 teaspoons vanilla extract

½ teaspoon grated lemon zest

1 teaspoon fresh lemon juice

¾ cup chopped walnuts

2 tablespoons powdered sugar

Preheat the oven to 350°F. Butter and flour a 9 × 5 × 3-inch loaf pan.

Run the carrots and apples through a juicer. Reserve 2 cups of the mixed pulp and ¾ cup of juice.

Sift the baking powder, flour, nutmeg, cinnamon, and salt into a small bowl. In a separate bowl, beat the eggs into the brown sugar, granulated sugar, and oil. Stir in the mixed pulp. Gradually add the dry ingredients and the reserved juice until you have a smooth batter. Stir in the vanilla, lemon zest, lemon juice, and nuts, mixing well to make sure the nuts are evenly distributed. Pour the batter into the prepared loaf pan.

Bake until a toothpick inserted into the middle comes out clean, about 45 minutes. Allow the cake to cool in the pan before removing. Then dust with powdered sugar.

Note: If you do not have a juicer, you use 1½ cups grated carrot, ½ cup grated apple, and ¾ cup apple juice.

RASPBERRY ORANGE BUBBLY

Serves 8

The last day of Kwanzaa is a day of reflection, but it's also a day of celebration, for the first of the year always means a new beginning. Here's a celebration drink with which to toast friends and family with a vow to do better and be better in the coming year. Those who do not drink alcohol can substitute ginger ale for the sparkling wine and still have a wonderful punch.

¼ cup frozen raspberries

2 cups fresh orange juice,

1 (750 ml) bottle prosecco, sparkling
   wine, or ginger ale, chilled

In a blender, puree the frozen raspberries.

In a pitcher, gently stir together the raspberry puree, orange juice, and prosecco. Serve in champagne glasses. Toast the future and your hopes for it.

PROJECT: PERSONAL VOWS

Knowledge is like a garden:
if it is not cultivated, it cannot be harvested.
—Guinean proverb

THE PROJECT FOR THIS final day of Kwanzaa is one that places its emphasis on the Nguzo Saba of Imani (faith). It is one that looks ahead not only to the coming year but also to the larger future. Each individual in the family should pledge to make a positive change of one thing in themselves and/or in their community in the upcoming year. It may be something as small as cleaning up a room or a vow to get better grades, start that business you've been talking so much about, or just to start looking for the job that you really want. You may vow to be a better friend, to keep in better touch with family, or to try to be a kinder and more thoughtful person. It may be a vow to work with a community organization or even a vow to start one with your neighbors for the betterment of your community. You may just promise to try to learn one new thing, no matter how small, each day for the upcoming year. That's a vow we all should make. Write them down and place them in an envelope here, in this book. Next year, when Kwanzaa comes around, open the envelope and recall your vows. Will you have accomplished them? Has it been successful? What better way to end the holiday than with a promise to grow and learn.

Happy Kwanzaa
Kwanzaa yena iwe na heri

ACKNOWLEDGMENTS

First thanks must be given to Maulana Karenga. Had he not seen the need for a holiday that gives us as a people a time for reflection, renewal, and rebirth, there would be no Kwanzaa.

Thanks then go to all of those who went before who brought us to the point where we can celebrate our strengths and heal our differences.

An old adage regarding friendships goes, "some for a reason, some for a season, some for a lifetime." When I look at the list of those acknowledged in 1995, I am struck and saddened that many, too many, have become ancestors. I am equally struck by the steadfast constancy of most of the others and delighted by the fact that they have been joined by new friends, co-conspirators, and adopted family now too numerous to list by name. Instead, I'd rather celebrate all who have come, dined, collaborated, advised, cried, aided, laughed, and loved over the years. I am blessed with an international and still growing host of friends and relatives. I am grateful to them all as they are the bedrock of my life.

Some people though must be acknowledged by name. Thanks are due my support team: assistants Lily Smith and Noa Wiener; friend/adviser Lorin O. Lewis; superman of the mail, Eddie Garcia; cat sitter Julia Payne Hall; and friends and house wranglers Lionel Whiteman and JJ in New York and Rhonda Conley on Martha's Vineyard. I am grateful to Carla Hall for writing the foreword and for being a guardian angel as I entered a different phase of my writing career. My pit bull researcher daughter, Patricia Hopkins, is still only a phone call away and Kerry Moody is simply my brother from another mother.

My former editor, Sydny Miner, and my former agent, the late Carol Abel, who midwifed this work in 1995 must also be mentioned. My current agent, Susan Ginsburg, has over the years become my best friend and an important family member. Her assistant, Catherine Bradshaw, is quite simply invaluable. The Scribner team is truly amazing, especially senior production editor Laura Wise, who has the patience of Job. Kathy Belden, my current editor, is my sister/friend. She has now held my hand through three books, nurtured me through COVID, made me a PEN award finalist, and a *New York Times* bestseller; I have no words with which to thank her.

Kwanzaa ends with *Imani* (faith), so I too must end my acknowledgments by thanking the Creative Spirit. Without guidance from divine hands nothing I do would get done.

Aśè

INDEX

ABOUT THE AUTHOR

JESSICA B. HARRIS is the author of twelve cookbooks documenting the foods and foodways of the African diaspora. She has lectured widely in the United States and abroad and has written extensively for scholarly and popular publications. Harris consults internationally for institutions including the New York Botanical Garden, the Martha's Vineyard Museum, the Oxford Cultural Collective, and the Smithsonian Museum of African American History and Culture, where she conceptualized the Sweet Home cafeteria. Her book *High on the Hog* is the basis for the Netflix series of the same name, which has won a Peabody Award and two NAACP Image Awards. Currently, Harris sits on the Kitchen Cabinet at the Smithsonian Museum of American History and is a trustee of the New York Botanical Garden.

Harris has been the recipient of many honors, including an honorary doctorate of humane letters from Johnson & Wales University and lifetime achievement awards from the Southern Foodways Alliance, the James Beard Foundation, and the Family Reunion. In 2021, she was named one of *Time* magazine's 100 Most Influential People in the world. Harris is professor emeritus at Queens College/CUNY where she taught for five decades. She divides her time between New York, Martha's Vineyard, and New Orleans.